SMITHFIELD

THE LONDON WOOL EXCHANGE

THE BALTIC EXCHANGE

SPITALFIELDS

THE FUR EXCHANGE

THE LONDON COMMODITY EXCHANGE

THE CORN EXCHANGE

POULTRY MARKET

THE METAL EXCHANGE

THE TEA MARKET MINCING LANE

BILLINGSGATE

WITHDRAWN
UTSA LIBRARIES

D0772601

KENWELL ROAD

OLD STREET ROAD

CITY ROAD

SHOREDITCH HIGH ST

BETHNAL GRN

CHARTERHOUSE STREET

ALDERSGATE ST.

CURTAIN

COMMERCIAL STREET

CANBU

FARN. VIADUCT

NEWGATE

ST. MARTINS LE GRAND

MOORGATE

BPS

HOXYAXE

POOL

STREET

RN-VIADUCT

RINDONS' RD

LUDGATE HILL

NEW BRIDGE ST.

CHURCHYARD

ST PAULS

CHEAPSIDE POULTRY

PRINCES STREET

BANK of ENGLAND

THREADNEEDLE ST

CORNHILL

LEADEN HALL ST.

ALDGATE

CANNON

QUEEN VICTORIA

STREET

LOMBARD ST

KING WILL ST

GRACECHURCH STREET

FENCHUR

EASTCH

BLACKFRIARS BRIDGE

SOUTHWARK BRIDGE

LONDON BRIDGE

EASTCH

TOWER HALL

TOWER

EASTSMIL

A M E S

SOUTHWARK STREET

TODLEY STREET

TOWER BRIDGE

BLACKFRIARS RD

SOUTHWARK BROAD ST

BOROUGH HIGH ST.

ENGLAND'S MARKETS

The Story of
Britain's Main Channels of Trade

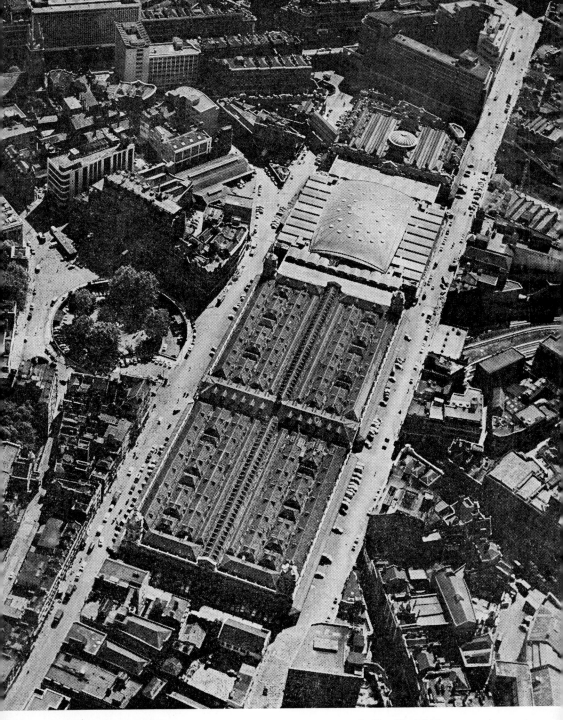

SMITHFIELD MARKET   A. Handford Ltd.

ENGLAND'S
MARKETS

The Story of
Britain's Main Channels of Trade

MARY CATHCART BORER

Illustrated with photographs

Abelard - Schuman

London - New York - Toronto

BY THE SAME AUTHOR:

COVENT GARDEN

© Mary Cathcart Borer 1968
First published in Great Britain 1968
Reprinted 1970
Standard Book Number 200 71519 4
First published in U.S.A. 1969
L. C. C. Number 69-10323

LONDON
Abelard-Schuman
Limited
8 King Street WC 2

NEW YORK
Abelard-Schuman
Limited
257 Park Avenue South

TORONTO
Abelard-Schuman
Canada Limited
1680 Midland Avenue
Scarborough

CONTENTS

INTRODUCTION

BUYING AND SELLING

It is a strange thought that the Englishman's traditional breakfast is eggs and bacon, since the hen is said to have first come into existence in the Far East, and the pig was not considered worth eating in this country until the eighteenth century, when strains to improve the native breed were imported from China and the Mediterranean.

Today, to the most ordinary homes in England, come commodities from the farthest corners of the earth—wheat from Canada, meat from the Argentine, wool from Australia, cotton from the Sudan, tea from Ceylon, rubber from Malaysia, petroleum from the Middle East. The list is endless. The business of importing and selling all these things, with a minimum of transport charges and a maximum of speed, is due to skilful methods of marketing.

In the early days of English history, when the people were self-supporting for the necessities of life, food and materials for clothing, pots and pans as well as household utensils still had to be marketed. Markets for the exchange of these goods came into existence at small towns which could easily be reached by roads or rivers.

From the earliest medieval times, there were laws to see that the prices of the goods being sold were fair. How many eggs, for example, could be considered a fair exchange for a basket of fish? There was a market court, and strict rules were made and enforced about the quality of the goods sold in the markets. So customers were protected against anyone who tried to palm off bad food, short measure or inferior workmanship.

Taxes, known as market tolls, were charged to cover the cost of this supervision. People were not allowed to trade without a licence. But these charges were as much to the advantage of the people who bought in the market as to the people who collected the taxes. Originally, permission to hold a market rested with the King, and market tolls were collected by the local sheriff. In medieval times, new towns were built. Henry II founded Woodstock, Richard I Portsmouth, and King John Liverpool. The Bishop of Worcester founded Stratford-upon-Avon, and the Bishop of Salisbury planned the new Salisbury, close to ancient Sarum. They invested in these towns. As well as deriving revenue from rents, they also obtained money from tolls and market dues. This second source was most profitable. In fact, the first important thing to do when a new town was being planned, was to see that it was granted a royal licence to hold a market.

When England began to import goods on a large scale, the same system of controlled marketing was used. London was its first big importing city, and its earliest quay was at Billingsgate, where tolls have been collected on various goods since 980 A.D.

During the nineteenth century, Great Britain was the hub of a vast empire. Her manufactured goods were sent all over the world, in exchange for raw materials and food. London was the financial centre of the world. And Britain is still the traditional pivot for marketing many of the world's basic commodities.

The London gold market is the focal point for dealings in gold. The Baltic Exchange, as well as being a market for shipping and air transport, is an important international market for grain, seeds and vegetable oils. The London Corn Exchange and the Liverpool Corn Exchange deal with homegrown produce, and are also international markets for a variety of agricultural products. The London Metal Exchange is the largest market in the world for copper, tin, lead and zinc. The London Fur Market is still the most important in the world, in spite of its European and American rivals.

The London Commodity Exchange has large and important markets in cocoa, coffee, copra, rubber and sugar. It has also smaller but valuable markets in many other commodities, such as essential oils and a large variety of spices. The London Wool Exchange is still a very important market for wool.

There is hardly any commodity which cannot be traded through an intermediary in Great Britain, from foreign stamps, for which London is the world's most important market, to almost priceless paintings, and other works of art, both modern and antique. During recent years London has become the most important city for art dealers.

In this book, I am first going to describe five of London's oldest food markets, and then some of the commodity markets, which have developed through the centuries. Their histories are fascinatingly varied, but the underlying principles of their business methods are the same. Among all of them is to be found Great Britain's richest heritage, the tradition that "our word is our bond." Once a seller and buyer have come to an agreement, even though no word is committed to paper, they will always observe the agreement.

MEAT

SMITHFIELD

Smithfield is the largest meat market in the world. It is the principal market for the meat and poultry of Great Britain, Ireland, the Commonwealth, Europe and South America. Yet many people who have lived in London all their lives have never seen it and have only a vague idea where it is. It lies in the northwest corner of the City of London. The best way to approach it is from the underground railway station of Farringdon. From there you turn left into Cowcross Street, which is not as rural as it sounds. It is lined on both sides with large, rather old-fashioned looking offices and warehouses, all connected with the meat trade.

Another left turn leads you to Charterhouse Street, where suddenly you are confronted—on the other side of the street—by the great arcade of the Central Meat Market, its imposing entrance surmounted by the arms of the City of London. It is a huge, red-brick building with stone pilasters. The tops of these form rounded arches which are

10

Smithfield Market, London

Photo: C.O.I.

filled in with delicate wrought-iron work to let in light and air. Below the arches a sloping glass roof projects over the surrounding pavement to form a covered way. At each corner of the market is a stone tower surmounted by a bronze cupola.

The building covers an area of three and a half acres. The architect, Sir Horace Jones, who planned the market, in the 1860's, was influenced by Sir Joseph Paxton's design for the Crystal Palace, which he built for the Great Exhibition in Hyde Park in 1851. Paxton was an engineer as well as an architect. He used prefabricated sheets of plate glass and prefabricated iron girders to enclose this large area. This idea was used in building the big railway stations and markets which were erected a few years later.

The Central Meat Market is really a gigantic shed. The arched entrance gives on to a wide, glass-roofed arcade, supported by slender iron columns and roof girders, all painted a bright sky blue. On either side there are lines of shops displaying neat rows of slaughtered animals. Crossing the central arcade at right-angles is another broad walk—the Central Avenue. From here, more lanes lead off on either side—row after row, stretching into the distance, each lined with butchers' shops, showing thousands of carcasses* of lambs and sheep, calves, cattle and pigs which hang from enormous meat hooks.

To the west of the Central Meat Market is the smaller poultry market, a modern building which has only recently replaced the Victorian market, after it was destroyed by fire. Farther west again, at the corner of Charterhouse and Farringdon Streets, is a general market. Here eggs, poultry, game, bacon and cheese, as well as more meat, are sold, but, of course, Smithfield's most important business is with meat.

The whole area of Smithfield Market, including the surrounding streets, where storage warehouses and cold stores have been built, covers more than ten acres. There are four hundred shops—which between them have two miles of frontage—where 9,000 tons of produce could be displayed at a time. There are thirty gates on to which four hundred four-ton trucks can be backed and loaded at one time.

* Animals' bodies without heads, limbs or offal.

There are about 3,000 people employed in the Market itself. A further six hundred porters are employed to carry the meat out of the Market. In addition, many thousands of people in the surrounding area work in the meat industry.

Smithfield is the wholesale meat market for at least eight million Londoners, and ninety per cent of the meat passing through the market is sold in London and its surrounding counties.

Like Billingsgate, Leadenhall and Spitalfields, Smithfield is a survivor of one of the ancient produce markets of the City of London, and is owned by the City Corporation. It is a free market. Goods are laid out on display. They are bought on the spot and carried away to the buyers' retail shops, hotels or restaurants.

Supplies of beef, mutton, lamb, pork and poultry slaughtered in Great Britain and Ireland arrive by motor and rail, and the imported produce comes from ships unloading at London Docks, or from the cold stores at the Docks or near the market. The amount of produce which passes through the market is enormous. In an average year it amounts to 400,000 tons. Rather more than half of this comes from Great Britain and Ireland. Most of the imported beef is from the Argentine, and the imported mutton and lamb from the Commonwealth countries, principally New Zealand.

It was nearly a hundred years ago, in 1876, that the first consignments of frozen meat arrived in Smithfield from the Argentine, after Charles Teller's important discovery of refrigeration. Refrigeration enabled the ranchers in South America, who had too much meat, to sell it to Britain, where an increasing population was creating a shortage of meat, and making it too expensive for the poorer people to buy. Very soon, cold stores were built at Smithfield, under the Market, and in the streets nearby. The Port of London Authority also built cold stores in Charterhouse Street and St. John Street, as well as at the Royal Docks, where most of the imported frozen and chilled meat arrives. Frozen meat is quite hard and can be kept for fairly long periods, but it must be thawed before it can be cooked. Chilled meat, which is not so deeply frozen, is brought straight from the ship to market.

The frozen meat stores, adjacent to Smithfield, can house 15,000 tons of frozen meat, so if there should be any hold up of supplies, through a strike, or any unforeseen disaster, there is always a reserve on which the Market traders can draw. London imports rather less quantities of chilled and frozen mutton and lamb than it did before the last war. About three times more chilled beef is imported than frozen.

Until the end of the eighteenth century, Britain was self-supporting in food and her imports were mainly luxuries. Her position changed during the nineteenth century. She acquired a vast empire of un-developed lands in Canada, Australia, New Zealand and South Africa, while the invention of power-driven machinery brought about the industrial revolution. At the same time, improved standards of living led to a massive increase in the birth rate. Important dis-coveries in medicine and surgery reduced the death rate. In 1800 there were less than nine million people in England and Wales. By 1900, the figures had increased to thirty-two million. In 1939 it was about forty-six million. Since then, it has gone up by another six million to over fifty-two million.

At the beginning of the nineteenth century, Britain was mainly an agricultural country, but the development of machinery turned it into an industrial country. Cheap food was imported from the pioneer countries of America and the Empire to feed the rapidly increasing population. During these years the City of London prospered. Since Britain was the first country to become industrial-ized, she became not only the workshop of the world but also the world's market for many important commodities. Now other nations have caught up or superseded her. Her old customers no longer need so many of her exports, nor have they so much surplus food to sell, because their own populations have increased.

Britain, today, imports half her foodstuffs, mainly from North and South America, Canada, Australia, New Zealand, Eire, Den-mark, the Netherlands, France and South Africa. This represents forty per cent of the value of her imports. The rest consists mainly of petroleum and oil, and the basic materials for manufacturing. In return, more than five-sixths of her exports are manufactured goods. Of these, nearly half are engineering products.

Though Britain is such a densely populated and industrialized country today, agriculture is still one of her largest and most important industries. 49,000,000 acres of her 60,000,000 acres of land are still farm and grazing ground. Each year this area becomes a little less, as towns and industries spread over the countryside. But the loss of agricultural acreage has been compensated by the new, scientific methods of farming and animal rearing, which have increased productivity.

The production of British beef is greater than it was before the war, and less beef is imported. British pastures have always produced exceptionally good sheep. In medieval times the country's wealth was founded on the large exports of English wool. Now wool is again becoming important to English sheep farmers, although their main business is producing fat lambs for market. The production of pigs for bacon, pork and sausages is steadily increasing. The people now eat more than twice as much pork in one form or another than they did before the war.

There has also been a great increase in the poultry flocks in recent years. In 1964, 150,000,000 birds were bred. At the same time, scientific techniques have nearly doubled a hen's yield of eggs. One bird can now be expected to lay two hundred eggs in a year. This means that, today, nearly all the eggs eaten in Britain have been home-produced.

The Corporation of the City of London runs Smithfield as a service for meat producers who want to sell their produce. The market pays for itself, but the market authority does not set out to make a profit. It charges rent for the shops on the basis of the number of square feet occupied, and exacts a toll of one farthing* for every 21 lbs of goods passing through the markets, which works out at 2s 3d a ton.

Most of this money goes to the upkeep of the market and its administration. This includes the maintenance of the thirty men who make up the Market police force. Their chief duty is to see that all

* A quarter of 1d.

5

the bye-laws are kept. Any surplus money which then remains goes into a special account which is known as the City's Cash. The City's Cash is used for a number of purposes. Banquets to entertain distinguished foreign visitors to the City are an important item. Then the City owns certain open spaces, in and around London, such as Epping Forest, which are preserved for the pleasure of her citizens. The maintenance expenses of these open spaces, including the salaries of the forest wardens, are paid out of the City's Cash.

As Smithfield is an open market, anyone with a good trading reputation may rent a shop there. Four types of firms are in operation. First, there are the commission salesmen. Consignments of home-killed meat are sent to them, which they sell for the highest price they can get. The money from these sales is returned to the sender of the goods, less a selling commission of about five per cent.

Then there are the importers, who buy and slaughter the cattle abroad. They bring the shipments to Smithfield for sale. This group represents world-wide organizations, such as Swift and Armour, who not only produce, but refrigerate, pack and store their own meat. There are about eighty of these big wholesalers in the Market, and they each occupy several shops. The third group consists of the firms who buy either live or slaughtered stock directly from the farmer or his agent. This is possibly the riskiest type of marketing, from a wholesaler's point of view, for the day-to-day price of meat is governed by the daily changes in supply and demand.

The fourth group are known as jobbers or middlemen. They buy meat in bulk in the Market and re-sell it to the ordinary retail butchers. Of course, some firms deal in more than one of these types of marketing.

Smithfield is also a factory. In the old days, the butcher himself would carve up a slaughtered animal into loins, legs, shoulders and other cuts, which people buy for cooking. The spare, awkward bits would be used to make pies and sausages. But today, eighty per cent of the meat is cut up at Smithfield, into what are known as primary joints. These are bought by the retail butchers and cut into the smaller handier joints which they sell to the customers in their shops. The

16

rest of the meat is bought by big manufacturing firms such as Dring's and Wall's and used for meat pies and sausages.

In theory, because Smithfield is an open market, it should be possible to go to any of the shops and buy, say, a lamb chop. But in practice there would be difficulties. Smithfield is essentially a wholesale market. Therefore, the butchers who cut up the primary joints would not have the necessary time to prepare a properly trimmed lamb chop, which you would buy at a good retail butcher's shop.

All sales in the market are by "Private treaty". This means that the salesman determines the fair price to charge. The buyer either agrees to it, or decides not to buy, or he may try to persuade the salesman to reduce his price. But once both parties have agreed on the price, they will always abide by their word. This is part of the tradition of integrity which persists in all the dealings between merchants of the City of London, and which is often the wonder and envy of visitors from abroad. It has been said that this tradition is gradually breaking down in certain businesses in the City, but at Smithfield there are no defaulters.

At the end of the morning's business, the prices charged for the various goods, and the quantities which have been sold, are sent to the Superintendent's office. This is high up at the top of the staircase near the main entrance, overlooking the shops of the Central Arcade. Here the highest and lowest prices which have been paid for the various commodities are extracted from the reports. At 1.30 p.m. each day, they are shown on the notice board in the market entrance, together with the amount of tonnage which has been sold on the previous day. These figures are also sent to Reuter's News Agency, for the price of meat at Smithfield is of world importance, and affects world prices.

Smithfield is opened at midnight for the delivery of produce. The lorries begin to arrive in the late evening, and continue in a never-ending stream all through the night. Meat comes by road or rail, from slaughterhouses all over the British Isles. Most comes all the way by road. In fact, more than eighty per cent of the tonnage of Britain's freight traffic moves by road. The railways, in an attempt to try and regain some of this trade, have recently introduced special container freight trains for meat. These run from stations near the slaughter-houses directly to the London goods' depots, where the containers are transferred to road vehicles. This saves a great deal of work in handling the meat, and makes for less traffic congestion on the main roads.

While the fresh meat is arriving at the market from the slaughter-houses, the frozen and chilled meat is being brought in from the cold stores and docks.

Two types of manual workers are on duty at this time, both night workers, for the job can take place only during the early hours of the morning. There are the "pullers-back" who heave the meat from the inside of the vans on to the tail-boards.* Then the "pitchers" take over. Their job is to carry the meat from these vans to the tenants' premises, and hang them on the giant meat hooks. It is extremely heavy work, and it sometimes takes three pitchers to carry one large carcass of beef.

The pitchers are usually finished by about four o'clock in the morning. By this time, the highly-skilled "cutters" are at work, cutting the meat into huge, primary joints. Helping them are the "humpers," who move the meat about within the shop, and the weighers or "scalesmen" who keep a record of the weights of all the joints.

The salesmen arrive at about half-past four. They see that every-thing is in order for the morning's business. During these hours, health inspectors employed by the Corporation of London can be expected at any time, to ensure that the meat is up to the high Smithfield standard.

By five o'clock, the first buyers arrive. They are of all sorts, from ordinary retail butchers to people buying for the big organizations such as the supermarkets, buyers from the large hotels, like the Savoy, or from London stores which have famous food departments, as, for example, Harrods.

By the time they have finished buying, they may have acquired a

* Hinged or removable part of vehicles.

side of beef from the Argentine, another from Scotland, veal from Holland, sheep and lambs from New Zealand, pork from Ireland, rabbits from Australia or China, poultry from the Home Counties* and game from the North of England and Scotland.

The organization for removing this produce from the market is as efficient as the process of delivering it. Buyers may have their own lorries waiting outside the market. Then all they have to do is to hire one of the special porters, known as "bummarees",† to load them. Otherwise, there are firms of carriers, associated with the market, who will undertake the transport for them. Their clerks have desks under the glass awning outside the market. The buyer tells a clerk what he has bought, from which shops and where he wants his purchases sent. The clerk then orders one of his firm's porters to collect these goods, load them on to a van owned by his firm, and send it to its destination.

There are about a hundred and thirty "bummarees" at Smithfield, and they are all self-employed. They provide their own white caps, overalls and trucks. They wear red-and-white arm badges, to distinguish them from the other market porters, who wear different coloured badges. Until recently, the "bummarees" used to wait for work under the clock in the Central Arcade. Now a clerk has been appointed to organize them, and see that they have a regular flow of work. The "bummarees" are paid by the person hiring them, according to an approved scale of charges based on the weight carried.

All porters must be licensed each year. They earn very good money while they are young and strong, but the work is extremely hard. They begin at half-past four in the morning and go on until buying stops at about one o'clock in the afternoon. Nevertheless, sons often follow in their fathers' footsteps, and the family tradition of the son

---

* Counties surrounding London.

† The name "bummaree" is said to have survived from the old days of sailing ships, when fishing smacks—becalmed in the Thames estuary—were unable to reach Billingsgate quickly with their perishable cargoes of fish. In those days, bumboat men used to row out to the fishing boats, buy the fish, row it ashore, and make their way to Billingsgate by a horse and light cart. Another explanation of the term is that it is a corruption of *bonne maree*, which means "good fresh fish."

doing the same work as his father before him persists all through the market.

At one o'clock trading stops. By about two o'clock in the afternoon, there is practically nothing left in the market. The market traders are able to judge pretty accurately how much they are going to sell each day, and like to see their shops empty by closing time.

When business is over for the day, the salesmen and buyers have departed, and the porters are taking a well-earned rest in one of the innumerable pubs and cafés surrounding the market, the cleansing gangs move in. They sweep and hose the market in preparation for the thousands of freshly slaughtered animals which will be arriving some eight hours later, in time for the next day's business.

Smithfield market stands on historic ground, for cattle have been bought and sold here since early medieval times. On the south side of the market, in West Smithfield, is St. Bartholomew's hospital, which was founded by Rahere, a Canon of St. Paul's Cathedral, and also Rahere's beautiful Norman Church of St. Bartholomew the Great.

Smithfield was once known as the "Smooth" field. It was just outside the City walls, but within its jurisdiction. A horse fair was held there every Friday. Horses, cattle, sheep and pigs were bought and sold, and it was known as the King's Market.

Rahere lived during the reign of Henry I and was popular at Court. In his young days, he was very gay and worldy for a Canon. Then tragedy came to the Court, for the King lost his only son in the wreck of the White Ship and was heartbroken. Rahere was saddened and sobered by the King's unhappiness and went on a pilgrimage to Rome. On the way, he fell desperately ill. As he was recovering he had a dream in which he was visited and comforted by a vision of St. Bartholomew. Rahere determined that when he returned home he would build a hospital for the poor citizens of London and also a church. The King agreed to his plan and granted him the site of the King's Market, with its valuable market tolls.

Rahere founded the Augustine priory of St. Bartholomew in 1123, and about the same time the famous hospital. Pilgrims used to visit the priory, particularly during the times of the Church festivals. Hucksters and vendors of all kinds always appeared on these occasions and Smithfield began to take on the appearance of a fairground. This was how St. Bartholomew's fair began. In the early days, it was mainly a cloth fair, and the drapers and clothiers used to keep their wares inside the priory walls at night for safety. The names of the quiet little streets round Smithfield's ancient and lovely church—Cloth Fair, Cloth Court, Barley Mow Passage and Rising Sun Court—are all reminders of the old fairground.

The priors of St. Bartholomew were the Lords of the Fair for many years, which meant that they received the fair tolls. But when the power and wealth of the monasteries were curtailed, the City Fathers stepped in and claimed this income. The weekly horsemarket was still held and on other days Smithfield was used for tournaments and archery contests.

It was also a place for public executions. During Mary Tudor's short reign, at least two hundred Protestants were burned there for their religious convictions.

During the reign of Charles I, the City of London finally took full control of Smithfield and organized it as a market place for live cattle. The area was paved and enclosed with railings. Monday was the day for fat cattle and sheep; Tuesday, Thursday and Saturday mornings were for the sale of hay and straw and the afternoons for horses and donkeys; while on Fridays, cattle, sheep and milch cows were sold.

A large number of these animals were slaughtered in West Smithfield and the meat was sold by the butchers of Newgate market, just on the other side of the hospital. But as London grew, more and more buildings crowded round this corner of the City, and it became increasingly unsuitable for a cattle market. Conditions for the animals were appalling and they suffered terribly. Dickens gives a grim description of Smithfield market in the middle of the last century in *Oliver Twist*.

". . . the ground was covered nearly ankle-deep with filth and mire, and a thick steam perpetually rising from the reeking bodies of the cattle, and mingling with the fog which seemed to rest upon the chimney-tops, hung heavily about. All the pens in the centre of the large area, and as many temporary ones as could be crowded into the vacant space, were filled with sheep; and tied up to the posts by the gutter-side were long lines of oxen, three or four deep. . . . The whistling of drovers, the barking of dogs, the bellowing and plunging of beasts, the bleating of sheep, and grunting and squeaking of pigs; the cries of hawkers, the shouts, oaths and quarrelling on all sides, the ringing of bells, and the roar of voices that issued from every public house, the crowding, pushing, driving, beating, whooping and yelling . . . rendered it a stunning and bewildering scene, which quite confused the senses."

Newgate market, where the meat was sold, was not much better, as it was both a retail market and also the place where meat arrived from all over the country. All this business was crowded into far too small an area. "Through the filthy lanes and alleys no one could pass without being either butted with the dripping end of a quarter of beef, or smeared by the greasy carcase of a newly-slain sheep. In many of the narrow lanes there was hardly room for two persons to pass abreast" wrote one visitor.*

In 1855, the City of London decided to move the cattle market from Smithfield to Islington, where proper slaughterhouses were built. They then built the meat market on the site and the traders from Newgate market moved in, with an impressive ceremony presided over by the Lord Mayor. A banquet was held in the Grand Arcade for twelve hundred people. Barons of beef and boars' heads were served by the Lord Mayor's footmen, after which the speakers expressed the hope that the new market would bring ample tolls to the Corporation, cheap meat to the people and profits to the salesmen.

St. Bartholomew's fair moved with the cattle to Islington and became known as the Caledonian market, a "flea" market where at one time many a bargain could be found amongst the quantities of of secondhand and antique goods for sale. Both the live cattle market

* *OLD AND NEW LONDON*. Edward Walford, Cassell, 1889.

and the flea market continued until 1939. But they closed on the outbreak of war, and never reopened. Several markets have appeared since in other parts of London, and some old-established ones have expanded, notably the Portobello Road market. The Islington slaughterhouses have now closed, so that there is no longer a large public slaughterhouse in London.

FISH

BILLINGSGATE

Billingsgate, the fish market, is the oldest of the City of London's ancient produce markets, for it has been used for the sale of fish for more than a thousand years. It is situated by the oldest quay in London, down on historic Thames Street, where Geoffrey Chaucer was born in the fourteenth century. It is now overlooked by the City Monument, which was built close to the spot where the disastrous fire of London broke out on the fateful September morning of 1666. Through the years, Billingsgate has become not only the largest wholesale fish market in Great Britain, but also the most important inland wholesale fish market in the world.

The early Celtic settlement, on the site which was to become the City of London, was built on the first slightly rising ground above the marshy wastes of Essex, where the little stream of the Walbrook joined the Thames. The Walbrook has long since been filled in, but this part of the Thames has become the busy Pool of London. The

24

BOX CHARGED 5/-
RETURN TO
ABERDEEN

Photo: C.O.I.

Celtic village was only a few dozen mud huts, surrounded by an earth wall, and they called it Llyn-Din, the Hill by the Pool. About 400 B.C. Belin, the Celtic King, rebuilt the wall. On the south side, along the river front, he ordered a small landing place to be cut, with a wooden quay. To enter the city from the quayside, a watergate was made in the wall, which was called Belinsgate, a name which, through the long centuries, has gradually changed to Billingsgate. The story goes that when Belin died his body was cremated and "the ashes set over the gate in a vessel of brass, upon a high pinnacle of stone."

When the Romans arrived in Britain, they chose the site of Llyn-Din for their first trading station, probably about A.D. 25, for at the spring tides the grey waste of marshes below this point was often submerged by the flood-waters. Llyn-Din, which was later to become known as London, was also far enough inland to be safe from pirates on the high seas. It was a convenient place from which the country could be explored, and the river was narrow enough to be forded.

After their invasion of Britain, in 43 A.D., the Romans remained for four hundred years. During all this time, Billingsgate was the quayside from which Britain's metals, wool and animal skins were exported to Rome. And such luxuries as furs, glass, silk, ivory and precious stones, from the faraway countries of the Roman Empire, arrived there in exchange.

When Rome fell and Britain was invaded by the Anglo-Saxons, London was almost deserted for many years, and her Roman buildings fell into ruin. The Anglo-Saxons disliked towns and preferred to live in isolated family groups scattered throughout the countryside. However, these dark ages came to an end when missionaries reintroduced Christianity to England. The missionaries were followed by the European traders, and England gradually began to take her part in European trade and commerce. Merchants moved into London, for they needed the Thames as a commercial highway, and Billingsgate became important again.

During the ninth century, King Alfred repaired the floodgates of

26

London and rebuilt the quay at Billingsgate. A general market developed, where such things as corn, coal, iron and steel, wine, salt and pottery, as well as fish were landed and sold. German and Flemish merchants brought wheat and rye, ropes, masts, wax and steel. The French merchants brought barrels of wine.

Eventually Billingsgate became better organized. About 1250, the German or Hanse merchants settled in their own quarter, known as the Steel Yard, a little upstream, where Cannon Street railway station now stands, and here they built their beautiful hall. The French wine merchants moved to a site close by, which was known as the Vintry, and here, facing on to Thames Street, the Vintners' Hall was eventually built. At Billingsgate, fish became the most important commodity sold.

During the reign of Edward I (1272–1307) fixed prices for the best soles at Billingsgate were 3d a dozen. Oysters were 2d a gallon and the best fresh salmon were four for 5/-.

The fishing industry, both in the rivers and at sea, was of great importance in medieval times. Fridays were fast days, when no meat was eaten, though fish was permitted. There were many other meatless days throughout the Church calendar, as well as Fridays.

Yarmouth was the most important fishing port during the Middle Ages, and Yarmouth herrings were already famous. English North Sea fishermen went as far afield as Iceland, where they opened trading stations. By the sixteenth century they had reached Russian waters, where they began a small whaling industry. Fishermen from Devon and Cornwall had followed the Atlantic explorers and, like the fishermen from France, Spain and Portugal, paid regular visits to the rich cod-fishing grounds off Labrador and Newfoundland. They must have invented some drying or salting process, so that the fish was still eatable by the time they reached England again.

In Tudor times (1485–1603), the fishing industry was given every protection and encouragement in England, for it was from the experienced seamen of the fishing fleets that the sailors of the Royal Navy were recruited in time of war.

After the Reformation in the Western Church, during the sixteenth century, which led to the establishment of the Protestant Church, fast days were no longer enforced in England for religious reasons. In fact it was declared illegal for anyone to insist that it was a religious duty to fast. However, in order to protect the fishing industry and maintain a supply of skilled seamen for the Navy, it was decreed that fish must be eaten on Fridays and during Lent, and there were penalties and fines for anyone who broke the law. After 1563 Wednesdays were also declared fast days, so that England then had more meatless days than any other country in Europe. These Fishing Acts created so much extra demand for fish that a thousand more men were brought into the fishing industry. All of them, said the report, would be available and "ready to serve in Her Majesty's ships."

At this time John Stow, London's sixteenth-century historian, wrote of Billingsgate: "It is a large watergate, or harborough, for ships and boats commonly arriving there with fish, both fresh and salt, shell-fishes, salt, oranges, onions and other fruits and roots, wheat, rye and grain of divers sorts, for service of the City and parts of the realm adjoining."

Fish was caught in large quantities in the Thames which in Stow's day produced at least half of London's fish supply. He wrote rapturously of its quality. "What should I speak of the fat and sweet salmons daily taken in this stream, and that in such plenty (after the time of the smelt is past) as no river in Europe is able to exceed it? But what store also of barbels, trouts, chevens, perches, smelts, breams, roaches, daces, gudgeons, flounders, shrimps, eels etc. are commonly to be had therein. . . ."

In addition to these supplies, fish caught in the Thames estuary and the North Sea was also brought to Billingsgate for sale to Londoners.

Until the end of the eighteenth century there was an important salmon fishery up-river at Putney. Even at the beginning of the nineteenth century, before the river was polluted by the discharge from gas works, sewage works and factories, fishermen were catching salmon, roach, plaice, smelts, flounders, eels, dace and dabs in the

Thames, in large enough quantities to make a living from their sale at Billingsgate.

As fish became an increasingly important item of food, so did the importance of Billingsgate as a fish market increase. By the end of the seventeenth century it was almost entirely a fish market. In 1699, an Act of Parliament made Billingsgate "a free and open market for all sorts of fish whatsoever, six days of the week, and on Sundays (before Divine service) for mackerel."

Until the middle of the eighteenth century roads were little developed in England. Wherever possible, goods were carried by water, either through the inland waterways of the upper reaches of the rivers, or from port to port along the coast by seagoing vessels. The first canals were built in the 1760's, but it was not until the turn of the century that Macadam's method of road-building was adopted and land transport became a practical proposition. So Billingsgate fish continued to arrive by water for many years to come. Then, early in the last century, came the development of the railways. About the same time, sail was gradually replaced by steam, and steam fishing trawlers came into operation. It was quicker for the trawlers to land their catches at the nearest ports, from which they could be speedily sent to Billingsgate by the new railways.

The quantities of fish being sent to Billingsgate by these new methods rapidly increased. But it found a ready market, as the population of London and the home counties was also rapidly increasing.

In 1876, the present fish market, designed as was Smithfield by Sir Horace Jones, was built at Billingsgate to replace the ancient sheds and stalls. Though smaller than Smithfield, it is similar in style, with a glass roof supported by iron pillars. It has a floor space of nearly an acre, and below are cold-storage chambers and workshops. Another subsidiary market for dry fish, with a floor space of about 5,000 square feet, called Billingsgate Buildings, was built opposite the Billingsgate Market in 1888.

The main fish market is surrounded by shops, and the floor of both Billingsgate and Billingsgate Buildings is divided into squares known as stands. There are over three hundred stands, which the holders lease from the market authorities. The Market Superintendent collects rents on a weekly basis, and also a toll of twopence for every hundredweight of fish sold. A hundred and thirty firms are represented in the market, and 2,500 people are employed, including five hundred licenced porters.

Up until 1936, occasional deliveries of fish were landed at Billingsgate by trawler, but today it all comes either by rail or by long-distance road transport. Fish from the North Sea fishing fleets is landed at the east coast ports and mostly sent by rail to Broad Street. From Scotland and the North of England it arrives at King's Cross station. From the west country it comes to Paddington. From these stations it is transferred to lorries which bring it to the market.

Large quantities of fish are also imported from Denmark, Norway, Sweden, Holland and Belgium, and most of this passes through the ports of Harwich and Newcastle.

The fishing industry in the United Kingdom today contributes only a quarter per cent to the national economy, but it is of great importance to Scotland and also to some of the major English fishing ports.

The industry is composed of three main divisions, white fish, herring and shell fish, and of these white fish are the most valuable. This includes cod, haddock, plaice, turbot and sole, all of which live on or close to the seabed, and pilchards, mackerel and sprats which live nearer the surface. All these fish are caught in distant waters, such as the shores of Iceland, and in the West Atlantic, Greenland, Bear Island and the north coast of Norway. Nearer home, in what are called "middle waters" they are fished round the Faroe Islands: and the "near water" grounds are the North Sea, the Irish Sea and off the coasts.

The herring fishing grounds are also in the "near waters," usually within sixty miles of land. Shell fish are also found in inshore waters. These include crabs, lobsters, shrimps, mussels, escallops, cockles and oysters.

The main fishing ports of England and Wales are Hull, Grimsby,

Fleetwood, Brixham, Milford Haven and Lowestoft for white fish and Great Yarmouth and Lowestoft for herrings.

In Scotland, white fish are landed at Aberdeen, Granton, Fraserburgh, the Moray Firth, the West coast and Shetland. Herrings are landed all round the Scottish coast, at Aberdeen, Fraserburgh and Peterhead in the east, Ullapool, Maillaig, Oban and Portpatrick in the west and Shetland in the north. The herring fishing ports of Northern Ireland are Ardglass, Portavogie and Kilkeel.

White fish are caught all the year round, but herring fishing is seasonal. In Scotland, the Shetland islands and the north-east coast of England, herring are fished during the summer; and off East Anglia, herring are landed at Lowestoft and Yarmouth in the autumn.

The distant water vessels operate mainly from Hull, Grimsby and Fleetwood. They are big ships, over 140 feet long. There are over two hundred of them in service today and they make voyages which usually last from between two and three weeks, but when they visit the Arctic circle they are away for longer than this. Since the introduction of freezer trawlers, fishermen have been going as far afield as the waters of Newfoundland, Labrador and Greenland. These vessels are sometimes at sea for as long as three months at a time. Their ships are also factories, for they fillet and freeze their fish immediately it is caught.

Experiments are now being made to find out whether it will be practical to fish in this way off South Africa, processing and freezing the fish as it is caught, and bringing it back to Britain. The results of a survey of these grounds by the White Fish authority, helped by one of the Navy's hydrographers, suggest that these distant waters may yield an abundant supply of fish for Britain.

The middle water fishing vessels are smaller than those fishing in distant waters. At the end of 1964, there were 434 in service. They make shorter journeys, which usually last only a few days, and very rarely over two weeks, though some go as far as the Faroes and Iceland region. Some of these middle-water vessels fish for herring with drift nets, and usually return to port each day.

The inshore fishing trawlers are smaller still and are very seldom at sea for more than two or three days at a time. Most of them return to port each day.

The fishing industry employs about 21,600 regular fishermen, and nearly 6,000 part-time workers. In 1964, British fishermen landed 817,000 tons of fish, worth about £54,000,000. Of this, cod accounted for 43%, haddock for 19% and plaice for 10% of the total value. The value of the shell fish landed amounted to £2,900,000.

Including fresh, frozen, salted and canned fish, Britain imported 225,000 tons, worth £67,000,000, and of this amount 45,000 tons, worth £29,000,000, was canned salmon. Other canned fish imports were valued at £11,200,000.

Not as much fish is eaten in Britain now as before the 1939 war. In 1964, consumption was estimated to be 17.6 lbs per person a year, but during the 1930's the figure was 21.8 lbs.

Research into new and improved methods of curing, kippering and canning fish and also quick-freezing are going on all the time. The business of quick-freezing fish has been steadily increasing since 1952, and today fifteen per cent of all the white fish caught by British fishermen is treated in this way. Much of it is exported. In fact, nearly half of British fish exports are in quick-frozen packages and their yearly value is now over £8,000,000. Though exports of herring are declining, these frozen packs find a good market in Europe.

A valuable by-product of the processing of fish is fish meal for animal food and for fertilizers. About 78,000 tons of white fish meal and herring meal are manufactured each year in Great Britain.

Fresh water fishing plays a relatively small part in the fishing industry. The principal catches are salmon, sea trout and eels. They are caught mainly in river estuaries and also a short distance out to sea. In England and Wales the value of salmon caught each year is about £200,000, but in Scotland it is nearly £1,500,000 and in Northern Ireland about £250,000.

When the fishermen land their fish at British ports it is sold by auction at the quayside. The buyers are the wholesale fish merchants.

They sell to inland wholesalers, arranging the despatch of the fish by train or road. Though there are large fish markets throughout the country, notably at Grimsby, Hull and Lowestoft, the bulk of the catches come to Billingsgate, which remains by far the most important inland wholesale distributing fish market. It handles between 350 and 400 tons each day, most of it during three hectic hours in the morning, from six to nine. This represents about an eighth of the total amount of fish landed each day in Britain.

Sometimes the port merchants send their fish to Billingsgate to be sold by their agents on a 5% commission basis. Alternatively, stall holders at Billingsgate may themselves have ordered fish from the merchants, which they then resell. A third method of business is for London merchants to employ agents at the ports to buy for them, direct from the trawler owners and fishermen.

The majority of traders in Billingsgate market sell only complete "packages" of fish. These are loads of between forty-two to eighty-four pounds, which remain intact from the coast where they are packed to their final destination. But some traders, known as "bummarees," will sell less than a whole package, to suit the smaller fishmongers.

Speed is essential in the marketing of fish. So efficient is the organization of Billingsgate, that it is more practical for fish to be sent to London and then redistributed to the home counties, than to send it directly from the ports to its ultimate destination. Even fish ports, which may be suffering from a temporary shortage, due to bad weather conditions or some change in the population of the fishing grounds—causing a rise in prices—sometimes buy from Billingsgate. For here, with supplies coming from all over the country, and also from abroad, prices remain fairly stable.

The extra time taken in sending the fish to Billingsgate is slight, for fish leaving port on Monday is through Billingsgate and on sale in retail shops by Tuesday morning. But the advantages are many. Billingsgate merchants buy in such large quantities that they are in a better position to make purchases of the highest quality. Moreover, a retailer buying at the port, would have to take what he is offered, at the price he is asked. At Billingsgate he can see what he is buying and has a very wide range from which to choose, for the fish is drawn from every available source of supply. He can also bargain about the price.

Another very important advantage is that fish at Billingsgate is always inspected by representatives of the Fishmongers' Company. They are known as Fish Meters and they will reject any fish which they consider unfit for sale.

Obviously, the entire supply of 350 to 400 tons of fish on sale each day could not be on view at once. In any case, the stands at Billingsgate are quite small, averaging about sixty square feet, though some firms rent more than one stand. There are no marble slabs or benches. The stall is just a piece of red-tiled floor space. The rest of the floor is in black tiles. The salesmen therefore display only boxes containing samples of their wares. The tradition of integrity is so strong that a buyer can make his purchases with absolute confidence from the samples he selects.

After the fish has been landed at the fish ports and sold, it is quickly loaded on the waiting fish trains or lorries, which are timed to arrive at Billingsgate by about 5 o'clock in the morning. Often they are delayed until the last minute, so that the last of a fleet's catch can be picked up. Vans drive the fish from the main line stations to Billingsgate and they are parked in the new parking space which the Corporation of London has recently provided on the water front adjoining the market. Sample boxes are then unpacked and taken into the market for display. The vans are used as temporary warehouses for the bulk of the supply.

About 6 o'clock the retail buyers arrive. They park their vans in specially allotted parking spaces in streets as close as possible to the market.

They make their purchases by private treaty from the samples on view and receive tickets which will identify the different supplies which they have bought. These they hand to one of the fish porters, whose job it is to pick up the supplies and take them to the buyer's van. This is by no means as simple as it might sound, for there is no time to sort out supplies at the railway stations and the salesman's goods may be parked in more than one van.

The work has to be done as quickly as possible and the fish porter's job is a heavy and exacting one. Like the Smithfield porters, the men must be very strong, as the boxes of fish are extremely heavy. They sometimes have to carry loads of up to one and a half hundred-weight for distances of anything up to half a mile. They carry these loads on their heads, wearing distinctive leather hats for protection, and as a result they develop enormously strong neck muscles. The porters are all licensed and are famous for their speed and efficiency. Between them, they will sometimes shift three hundred tons of fish in less than three hours. As in the other City markets, there is a strong family tradition among them. Many porters' families have been in the service of Billingsgate for several generations.

By half past eight or nine o'clock in the morning, the selling for the day is over and the retailers are on their way back to their own shops, to sell their fish to the housewives. And at Billingsgate the cleansing squads move in to hose and sweep and make all ready for the following day's market.

POULTRY

LEADENHALL

The Superintendent of Billingsgate Market is also in charge of Leadenhall close by, the poultry market. Today it is a glass-roofed arcade of shops lying alongside Gracechurch Street and running between Fenchurch Street and Leadenhall Street, in the very heart of the City. It is one of London's most historic sites, for this was once part of Roman London.

Early in the fourteenth century, a mansion stood here in large grounds. The roof of the house was lined with lead, which in those days of plaster and timber dwellings was a remarkable innovation, and it was this feature which gave it the curious name of Leaden Hall. The owner was Sir Hugh Neville and he gave permission for a market to be held in the grounds, for the benefit of his tenants.

The market proved so successful that a hundred years later, when Sir Richard Whittington was mayor of London, the City Corporation acquired the site and became the lords of the manor of Leadenhall.

Photo: C.O.I.

A few years later, in 1445, after a series of bad harvests, the mayor for that year, Sir Simon Eyre, converted the mansion into a large granary, where grain was stored, so that in times of shortage the City always had a supply on which it could draw.

The rest of the space was an open market where meat, fish, poultry and vegetables were sold, as well as hides, wool, woollen cloth and metal goods. Gradually, however, Leadenhall market began to specialize in poultry and game and the dealers in other commodities moved to markets elsewhere.

Like Smithfield and Billingsgate, the present market was designed by Sir Horace Jones, and it was opened in 1881 as a wholesale poultry and game market. Business has changed since those times. The bulk of the wholesale poultry trade has now gone to Smithfield, so that Leadenhall has become mainly a retail market for general goods.

There are some seventy shops in the market, each occupying a floor space of approximately thirty square yards. About a quarter of the tenants now deal in poultry and game but there are also fishmongers, butchers, greengrocers and provision merchants, as well as a variety of other trading firms, including an electrician and a bookshop. All these merchants pay rent to the Corporation of London through the Market Superintendent of Billingsgate and Leadenhall. Records of sales are not kept and they do not pay market tolls.

With the city offices pressing close around it, Leadenhall is a surprising and attractive sight, especially at Christmas time. Then the poulterers' shops are crammed with turkeys from all parts of the country as well as from abroad. And during the grouse and pheasant shooting seasons, the rows of birds, forlorn as they may look, bring a breath of the moors and highlands to the City. On the Gracechurch Street side of the market are the fishmongers, who buy their supplies each day from Billingsgate.

Business flourishes at Leadenhall, as many of the shops specialize in provisioning the liners of the shipping companies for their journeys, including luxury cruises. Some also supply the numerous restaurants, clubs and canteens of the City.

Photo: C.O.I.

FRUIT AND VEGETABLES

1. COVENT GARDEN

Walk down any shopping street in a busy town far from the country-side and you will be sure to find a greengrocer's shop stacked with apples, bananas, lemons, oranges, tomatoes and, in the summer time, strawberries, raspberries, currants and peaches. Potatoes, cabbages, cauliflowers, onions, carrots and lettuces are always to be found.

Yet where do they all come from and how do they arrive at the greengrocers' shops, so far from where they are grown, in such an excellently fresh condition?

It is all due to an ingenious and highly efficient marketing system. Marketing has been defined as "all the operations involved in the movement of food from the grower to the consumer."

A greengrocer may sometimes obtain small supplies of, say, mushrooms or soft, summer fruit, from a local grower. But obviously it would be impractical for him to order a crate of oranges from

South Africa, bananas from the West Indies and lemons from Sicily each week.

The supplies of both home-grown and imported fruit and vegetables pass through the wholesale markets, at which merchants buy for distribution throughout the country.

Home-grown fruit and vegetables do not take up much of the country's agricultural land. It amounts to less than $2\frac{1}{2}\%$ of the large area of 30,000,000 acres under crops and grass, but the yield is very high and extremely valuable. In 1964–5, the total value of horticultural crops from the 400,000 acres of vegetables, and the 250,000 acres of fruit was £175,000,000 compared with the value of farm crops, which amounted to £334,000,000. Today, the average value of home-grown fruit and vegetables, including potatoes, is about £220,000,000.

Market gardening is carried on around all the large concentrations of population in the country, and in other places where the climate and soil are suitable for the particular types of fruit or vegetable.

Kent is one of the main fruit-growing counties for apples and pears, but they are also grown in large quantities in Cambridgeshire, Essex, Sussex, Worcestershire and County Armagh in Northern Ireland. About half of these are eating apples. The Cox's orange pippin is the most liked. The rest are cooking apples. Although the production of cooking apples is tending to decline in Northern Ireland, there are 8,000 acres of Bramley seedlings, still the best of the type. Cider apples for the cider-making industry are grown mainly in Devon, Herefordshire and Somerset. In these three counties there are 25,000 acres of cider apple orchards.

Plums come from Cambridgeshire, Gloucestershire, Kent, Norfolk and Worcestershire; cherries from Kent, raspberries from Perthshire and Angus; and blackcurrants in large quantities from Essex, Herefordshire, the Isle of Ely, Kent, Norfolk and Worcestershire. There are large strawberry farms in Cambridgeshire, Cheshire, Cornwall, Hampshire, Kent, Norfolk, Somerset and Worcestershire.

Salad crops, including beetroot, cucumbers, lettuce, mustard and cress, radishes, spring onions, tomatoes and watercress, are grown

41

in large quantities in the Lea Valley, where there are 700 acres of glasshouses, though in recent years production has declined. They are also grown in Hertfordshire, Worcestershire, Worthing and—in the north of England—in Lancashire and Yorkshire.

Britain has about 4,500 acres of glasshouses altogether, half of which are used for growing tomatoes. Each year between 75,000 and 80,000 tons of tomatoes are grown and the total value of all our glasshouse crops amounts to £30,000,000.

Peas, carrots, winter cabbage and potatoes are grown in very large quantities in the eastern counties, from Yorkshire to Essex. Early vegetables and tomatoes also come from the mild regions of Cornwall and the Channel Islands.

All this produce comes from intensive farming and a great deal of organic fertilizers are used. The larger farms have special packing sheds with washing and grading machinery to prepare the produce for market. Nowadays, many growers join co-operative groups. They send their produce to the group's packing station, to be graded and packed and the boxes marked with the grower's trademark, before being sent to market.

Although large quantities of apples are grown in Britain, many varieties are also bought from other countries. If you look at the table below you can see from which countries we import fruit and vegetables and at what times of the year.

CALENDAR OF FRESH FRUIT AND VEGETABLES

FRUIT

Apples – Argentina, Australia, Canada, France, Holland, Home Grown, Italy, Lebanon, New Zealand, South Africa, U.S.A.

Home Grown   July – Feb.
Imported   Throughout the year

Bananas – Brazil, West Cameroons, Canary Islands, Jamaica, Windward Isles and West Indies.

Imported   Throughout the year

Lemons – Cyprus, Greece, Israel, Italy, Morocco, Nigeria, South Africa, Spain	Imported	Throughout the year
Oranges – Argentina, Brazil, Cyprus, Jamaica, Israel, South Africa, Turkey, U.S.A.	Imported	Throughout the year
Peaches – Canada, France, Greece, Home Grown, Italy, South Africa, Turkey, U.S.A.	Home Grown Imported	June – Aug. Feb. - March June - Oct.
Pears – Argentina, Australia, Central Europe, Holland, Home Grown, Italy, New Zealand, South Africa, U.S.A.	Home Grown Imported	Jan. – Feb. Aug. – Dec. Throughout the year
Strawberries – Cyprus, France, Home Grown, Israel, Kenya, U.S.A.	Home Grown Imported	May – Sept. Jan. – June
Tomatoes – Canary Isles, Guernsey, Holland, Home Grown, Jersey, Spain	Home Grown Imported	April – Sept. Throughout the year

VEGETABLES

Brussels Sprouts – Home Grown	Home Grown	Sept. – March
Cabbage – Holland, Home Grown	Home Grown	Throughout the year
Red and White varieties Holland	Imported	Throughout the year

Carrots – Canada, Cyprus, Holland, Home Grown, Italy, U.S.A.	Home Grown Imported	Throughout the year Jan. – July
Cauliflower/Broccoli – France, Holland, Home Grown, Italy, Jersey	Home Grown Imported	Throughout the year Jan. – March, June, Nov. – Dec.
Cucumber – Canary Isles, Holland, Home Grown	Home Grown Imported	Feb. – Nov. Jan. – July, Sept. – Dec.
Lettuce – France, Holland, Home Grown, Italy, Jersey, Spain	Home Grown Imported	Feb. – Nov. Jan. – Aug., Oct. – Dec.
Onions – Argentina, Canada, Chile, Egypt, France, Holland, Home Grown, Hungary, Israel, Poland, South Africa, Spain, U.S.A.	Home Grown Imported	Sept. – Dec. Throughout the year
Peas – Home Grown, France	Home Grown Imported	June – Sept. May – June
Runner Beans – Home Grown	Home Grown	June – Sept.

POTATOES

Potatoes (*old*) – Home Grown only		Throughout the year
Potatoes (*new*) – Belgium, Canary Isles, Cyprus, France, Holland, Home Grown, Israel, Italy, Jersey, Malta, Morocco, Spain	Home Grown Imported	June – July Jan. – July Nov. – Dec.

44

Fruit growers in Israel, New Zealand, Australia, South Africa, the West Indies, the Mediterranean and the United States all have marketing organizations which are responsible for the grading, packing, shipping, distribution and advertising of the fresh fruit they export to the United Kingdom.

These organizations send the produce to the importers and wholesalers in the big British wholesale markets. The two most important of these markets are in London, at Covent Garden and Spitalfields. Other important London markets are at the Borough, Stratford and Brentford. Throughout the country as a whole, the main wholesale markets for fruit and vegetables are Brighton and Southampton in the south; Bristol and Cardiff in the west; Coventry, Birmingham, Derby, Nottingham and Wolverhampton in the Midlands; Wigan, Manchester, Halifax, Huddersfield, Bolton, Liverpool, Preston, Leeds, Bradford, Sheffield, Hull and Newcastle in the north; Aberdeen, Dundee, Glasgow, Edinburgh and Leith in Scotland and Belfast in Ireland.

These are known as primary markets. Importers either sell on commission for the growers, or buy outright from the growers for resale. The wholesalers usually buy from the importers though sometimes direct from the growers. Then they sell to the smaller or secondary wholesalers, who in turn re-sell to the shopkeepers. In this way the produce is distributed far more quickly and therefore arrives in people's homes in as fresh a condition as possible.

Home-grown produce is distributed in a similar way. It is despatched to the nearest primary market. The primary wholesalers sell to secondary wholesalers, who in their turn sell to the shopkeepers.

A large proportion of Britain's imported fruit arrives at the Port of London, which is still probably the busiest port in the whole world. Some of this produce, particularly the more exotic fruit, goes directly to the Foreign Fruit market at Covent Garden. There are warehouse facilities at the docks for the temporary storage of certain kinds of fruit. But the bulk of it goes to the warehouses of the London Fruit Exchange Brokers' Association at Spitalfields, which is only ten

45

minutes drive from the docks. Here it is sold by auction at the London Fruit Exchange.

Fruit—particularly apples, pears andall kinds of citrus fruits—are sold at the Fruit Exchange by sample, and the sample display room is on the ground floor of the building. Auctions are held twice a week up above the sample room, in the huge auction room. Catalogues are printed and the buyers mark them with the lots for which they intend to bid after inspecting the samples. All the buyers must be members of the Fruit Exchange and they include merchants from Covent Garden, Spitalfields and the Borough markets. The prices established at these auctions help the fruit traders all over the country to set their prices.

Covent Garden is the largest and most important of all the primary fruit and vegetable markets in the United Kingdom, and one of the largest in the whole world.

There has been a market on this spot, just north of the Strand, for hundreds of years. It was never one of the old City of London's produce markets as it lies well to the west of the City boundary. Seven hundred years ago this land, on the north side of the highway leading from London to the City of Westminster, was owned by the monks of St. Peter's Abbey and was described as seven acres of "fair spreading pastures." Part of it the monks used for a burying ground and the rest for a vegetable and fruit garden to supply the needs of their Westminster Abbey. In time, the monks began to sell their surplus crops to the citizens of London.

There were several vegetable markets within the City, including the Stocks market, where the Mansion House now stands, but the produce from the Convent Garden was well liked.

In course of time, the garden and the great field – the Long Acre – were enclosed by a brick wall. London was spreading beyond the confines of the City walls and along the river side of the Strand great mansions, such as Somerset House, Essex House and Suffolk House were built by members of the aristocracy. The produce of the Convent Garden became more popular than ever.

With the Reformation, the monks lost their garden. It became the property of the King, and in 1552 King Edward VI granted it to John Russell, the first Earl of Bedford.

For many years the Russell family did little to develop this land but their gardeners still tended the old garden and orchard and sold the produce. People from nearby villages began bringing their own produce to sell at what now became known as Covent Garden, and it gradually developed into a regular market place.

The Russells, at last, built Bedford House, facing the Strand, about where Southampton Street now runs. Then, early in the seventeenth century, they decided to develop the rest of their land. London was growing steadily and there was a great demand for new houses. Inigo Jones was commissioned to design the new housing estate. The old garden was dug up and the orchard destroyed. In its place, Inigo Jones designed a square surrounded by elegant town mansions. He planned the houses so that the first floors projected over the pavements and were supported by arches to make covered walks or arcades. Londoners had never seen anything like this before and were delighted with them. They called them, quite erroneously, "piazzas." It was the square itself which should have been called the piazza, but the arcades have been known as the piazzas to this day. The "piazza" on the south side was never built. For many years, this boundary of the square was the garden wall of Bedford House.

Four new streets led to the square, King Street, Henrietta Street, James Street and Russell Street, and Inigo Jones built St. Paul's Church on the west side, for the growing parish.

Covent Garden became a place of high fashion, the home of many members of the aristocracy and of several distinguished artists, as for example, Sir Peter Lely and later Sir Godfrey Kneller. This did not deter the market people. They now had more customers than ever and they spread their wares under the wall of Bedford House.

After the Civil War and the years of the Commonwealth came the restoration of Charles II. London became gayer and more populous than ever. More streets were built near Covent Garden, and now Drury Lane, Great and Little Queen Street and Bow Street became as fashionable as the piazzas. The first Drury Lane theatre was opened in 1663, and seven years later, Charles II granted the Earl of Bedford a charter to hold a market in the square.

Trade increased steadily and the market flourished. Many famous coffee houses were opened. As the squares of Mayfair were built to the west, the aristocrats moved into them and Covent Garden became the home of distinguished musicians and artists, theatre people and men of letters. The first Opera house was built in Bow Street in 1732, bringing more residents into the area, for people had to live close to their work in those days of horse transport.

The streets around the square were all very narrow and traffic soon became a problem, for there was a congestion of sedan chairs and carriages mingling incongruously with carts laden with market produce. But still the market grew.

Spitalfields market was as yet small and local. The Stocks market went to Farringdon Street, where it became known as the Fleet market, when it was removed in 1737 to make way for the building of the Mansion House. But it did not prosper. When the first Waterloo Bridge was opened, in 1817, Surrey and Kent growers took advantage of the easier way into London and brought their produce to Covent Garden instead of the struggling and decaying Fleet market.

The residents of Covent Garden were very soon protesting to the Bedford family and asking them to close the noisy market. But their pleas were in vain. So the residents gradually moved away and the market triumphed.

At last, in 1829, a proper market building was put up, designed by William Fowler. It consists of a central, covered arcade of double-storey shops, intersected by a similar arcade at rightangles. This building covers one and a half acres. The entrance, with its arch raised on two granite Tuscan columns and surmounted by a pediment bearing the Bedford coat-of-arms, matches the Tuscan portico of the church, and the market is surrounded by a covered arcade.

With the rapid increase of business during the 19th century, additional market premises had to be built. Previously, the flower market had been held in the open space in front of the church and around the entrance of the central arcade. Then the Floral Hall was built, alongside the Opera House, although it was never used for flowers, and today it is the Foreign Fruit Market. A flower market has been built in the southwest corner of the market, with an entrance in Wellington Street.

Today the market has spread relentlessly all round the square, into houses and streets which were built for a very different purpose, and it now covers some thirty acres. The Bedford family disposed of the market and trading rights of Covent Garden after the First World War. It was run by a company known as Covent Garden Market Limited for some time, but in 1961 the Government established the Covent Garden Market Authority, which now operates the market. They have control of six and a half acres. Their task is to improve existing market facilities or to find better ones.

The Authority has recommended that the market be moved to an eighty-acre site at Nine Elms, close to Vauxhall. The date suggested for the removal is 1970. There is a lot to recommend the move but many of the traders, whose families have worked in the market for three or more generations, do not welcome the idea.

It has now become a national fruit, vegetable and flower market. Produce from importers and home growers is sold to primary and secondary wholesalers, who distribute it throughout the country, as well as to retailers in the Greater London area.

There is such a big concentration of traders and buyers at Covent Garden and such a wide range of produce that the market is important in setting the prices for the whole country. About two hundred firms sell fruit and vegetables, either on commission or on their own account. Some are brokers or commission salesmen who sell the produce sent to them by the growers or overseas suppliers, at the best prices they can get. They take for themselves a fixed percentage of the proceeds. The commission salesmen usually have warehouse accommodation close to the market, where their goods can be inspected. Other market firms who buy and sell imported and home-grown produce on their own account, may also act as commission salesmen for other firms. There are also about forty firms selling the produce from their own orchards and market gardens, both at home and abroad, and some hundred firms selling flowers and plants.

As at Smithfield and Billingsgate, sales are by private treaty.

About 4,000 people are employed in and around the market, including 1,700 manual workers. Nearly 1,200 porters work in the fruit and vegetable section. 250 men are employed in the flower trade. There are about 150 "outside porters" who are self-employed and are used by the retailers to carry to their vans the produce they have bought in the market for their own shops.

It has been estimated that Covent Garden handles 30% of all the imported fruit, vegetables and potatoes which come into the United Kingdom and 7% of the total of home-grown supplies.

This represents £67,000,000 worth of produce, of which two-thirds in value—and a little over half in tonnage—is imported. Half goes to the shops of the Greater London area and the rest to provincial markets all over the country.

The flower trade market represents £10,000,000 of business each year. 90% of the flowers are home-grown, mainly in the Lea Valley, West Sussex, Lincolnshire, Cambridgeshire, the Channel Islands, the south and east coasts, Devonshire, Cornwall and the Scilly Islands. Most of them are sold to London florists or the flower shops in the near Home Counties of Surrey, Middlesex, Essex and Kent.

Throughout the night and early morning a thousand vans bring the produce to Covent Garden market. The goods arrive from the producing areas throughout the country, from the Port of London docks or from the London terminals to which it has been transported by rail from other ports, such as Dover, Harwich or Southampton.

Then the buyers arrive and nearly all the produce they buy is taken by road to its destination. This means that on a busy day 3,000 lorries are making their way out of the market into London's congested traffic between the City and the West End.

There are many ways in which Covent Garden has become maddeningly inconvenient. Yet everybody loves it for its romantic traditions and fascinating history, the unvaryingly high quality of its produce, the integrity of the traders and the unfailing cheerfulness of the porters. Many of these porters belong to families who have worked in the market for several generations, like the firms that employ them.

George Monro Ltd., recently celebrated their centenary in the market. They opened their business in North Row in 1862, and they now occupy one of the most interesting houses in the square, Number 43, King Street. Though the inside has been sadly altered, the frontage of this beautiful Inigo Jones house is still intact. It has had a succession of distinguished tenants, including the eccentric Sir Kenelm Digby, son of Sir Everard Digby, who was hanged for his share in the Guy Fawkes' plot of 1605 to blow up the British Parliament; Tom Killigrew, friend of Charles II and the first lessee of the original Drury Lane theatre; Admiral Russell, Lord Archer and James West—one of the presidents of the Royal Society. Then it became Evan's Hotel and Supper Rooms and finally, until 1933, when Monro's took it over, the headquarters of the National Sporting Club.

There is a kind of impertinent tenacity about the market in remaining so long in its old home and causing so many traffic jams. But there are many who will regret its passing, when the time eventually comes for it to move, and wonder what will take its place on this extremely valuable piece of land.

FRUIT AND VEGETABLES

2. SPITALFIELDS

Spitalfields market has a very different history from Covent Garden. It lies hidden away behind Bishopsgate, only a few yards to the east, down Brushfield Street. This area is just beyond the ancient city boundary and the Bishop's Gate, which once guarded its eastern approaches.

In the twelfth-century, the alderman of London who owned these fields offered them for the site of a priory and hospital. A silk mercer paid for their construction. The hospital was dedicated to the Virgin Mary and named St. Mary Spital (or hospital). It did good work right up until the dissolution of the monasteries and religious houses in the sixteenth century, by which time it is said to have had a hundred and eighty beds.

The priory and the hospital were pulled down but the hospital churchyard remained and with it the pulpit of Spital Cross, from which sermons were preached during Easter week, each year. The

Photo: Douglas Pike

Spital sermons were as famous as those preached from St. Paul's Cross, but during the Civil Wars the pulpit was destroyed.

Very little is known about the few residents of Spitalfields in those days. There were a few large houses built near the site of the old hospital and on a seventeenth-century map more houses are shown, built around a square field. It seems very likely that Spitalfields had already become connected with the silk-weaving industry by then as in 1682 a certain John Balch who was a silk thrower, or spinner, applied for a permit to hold a market in Spital Square twice a week.

Three years later, Louis XIV of France revoked the Edict of Nantes which had given freedom of worship to the French Protestants. They were henceforth regarded as outlaws and hundreds fled from the country, many crossing the Channel to England. A number of these Huguenots were skilled silk weavers and they came to Spitalfields to earn their living. Cottages were built to house them and their looms. Their skill was incomparable and they produced materials which were vastly superior to anything England had seen before. The silk weaving of Spitalfields became a flourishing industry and the population of the area rapidly increased, so that very soon there was a network of lanes and alleys covering the fields which had once surrounded the Spital.

Today the streets are shabby and run-down, but a few of the once elegant little houses of the Huguenot weavers still stand. Now they are mostly business premises although the intricate fan-lights and carved pediments of the front doors remain, and one can occasionally catch a glimpse of a beautifully carved oak staircase and an ornamental plaster ceiling. There were said to have been thirty-five French churches in London during the eighteenth century, of which eleven were in Spitalfields and Bethnal Green. The beautiful eighteenth century Christ Church, Spitalfields, which dominates the view as one walks down Brushfield Street from Bishopsgate, is now unsafe for worship, and a building close by is used instead. However, the vicarage adjoining the church is a wonderfully preserved example of early eighteenth century domestic architecture. It is all the more attractive because it is still the hub of active and constructive work in the parish.

By 1832, there were 50,000 people in Spitalfields dependent on the silk-weaving industry, with 14,000 to 15,000 looms at work. Their trade suffered from the competition of power looms, but the weavers refused to give up their handlooms and fell on hard times. By the end of the nineteenth century there were still a few weavers left, though they were ill-paid and desperately poor. They were very fond of singing birds and amused themselves with singing matches between their pet birds, which were timed by the burning of an inch of candle. For extra money, the weavers used to catch linnets, woodlarks, goldfinches and greenfinches, which were sold in Victorian London's street markets.

In his book *London's Markets*, written just over thirty years ago, W. J. Passingham describes coming by chance across a few elderly Flemish weavers living around Cranbrook Street in Bethnal Green, a little to the north of Spitalfields. They were still working at their complicated handlooms, making silk cloth for neckties and Jewish praying shawls. The weavers recalled their childhood days, when thousands of yards of expensive velvet and silk were being sent from Spitalfields all over the world and five hundred master weavers lived in Spital Square. It is very doubtful whether there are any weavers alive today and the art of hand silk-weaving has almost disappeared.

As the population of Spitalfields increased, so did the market. John Balch's market was taken over by a family called Goldschmidt. At that time it was a general market for fruit, vegetables, meat and poultry from the country districts only a few miles from the crowded parishes of Spitalfields, Shoreditch and Bethnal Green. The thrifty Huguenots introduced to Londoners, amongst many other things, the art of making ox tail soup. Previously, the market butchers had thrown away the tails, but the weavers, who were excellent cooks as well as skilled craftsmen, put them to good use.

There was a covered market building in Spital Square and the salesmen and other workers lived in houses surrounding it. But early in the eighteenth century, the market was burned down and was never rebuilt. Open stalls and ramshackle sheds were put up in its place. With the rapid growth of population during the nineteenth century, the demand for fruit and vegetables increased. Spitalfields developed into an important market for home-grown produce and did business seven days a week.

A young farm worker, Robert Horner, who as a boy had earned fourpence a week as a bird scarer for an Essex farmer, came to London to seek his fortune. He became a porter at Spitalfields market, worked hard, saved his money and before long was taken into partnership by one of the traders. In 1876, twenty years after his arrival in London as a penniless youth, he was in a position to buy the last few years of the lease of the market.

When the leasehold expired, he agreed to take out a new lease and rebuild the market. Business increased steadily. By the beginning of the present century it had far outstripped the facilities of the buildings Horner had put up. Then, in 1920, the Corporation of the City of London, which owned the freehold of the land, acquired the leasehold of the market. They realized the importance of Spital-fields as a market for home-grown produce as well as the increasing supplies of imported fruit and vegetables.

So Spitalfields became a City of London Corporation market like Smithfield and Billingsgate, and an extensive plan of expansion and reorganization began.

Horner's market had occupied three acres but the new main building extends over nearly five acres. It is surrounded by wide roads, and has thirteen broad crossroads inside. Each one is wide enough to take three vehicles abreast. Every stand in the market has at least one side fronting an internal road, so that produce can be loaded directly onto it. This saves an enormous amount of time, handling and porterage.

The market has upper floors and basements so that altogether there are nearly ten and a half acres of floor space for wares to be displayed and stored. Just before the last war the flower market was opened, where a number of wholesale flower and plant distributors have their stands. In 1965, the Corporation bought another building in Spital Square—now called Eden House—which has been converted into three large warehouses for the sale of fruit and vegetables.

In 1929, three years after the opening of the Liverpool Fruit Exchange, the magnificent London Fruit Exchange was opened, opposite the main market, in Brushfield Street. Until that time, and for a hundred years earlier, a large proportion of London's fruit had been auctioned at the City Sale Rooms, the business being in the hands of four firms of fruit brokers. These brokers handled much of London's fruit during Britain's nineteenth-century industrial expansion. But by the beginning of the twentieth century not only were people eating more fruit, but there were better and quicker communications with the fruit growing countries of the world. London then became a distribution point for fruit for the Continent as well as the United Kingdom.

By the 1920's the City Sale Rooms had become inadequate for the increased volume of business and the four fruit brokers joined forces with two other fruit brokerage firms to form a central fruit exchange for buyers and sellers.

In conjunction with the Central Markets Committee of the Corporation of London, these six firms organized and brought about the building of the London Fruit Exchange.

This building, which also houses the London Wool Exchange, has ample storage space for the fruit delivered from the docks. At the back of the building is a spacious vehicle parking area with room enough for trucks to back up to the loading bays. The customers are mainly wholesalers from East Anglia and the Home Counties, large retailers and men from the chain stores, commission buyers and small, wholesale merchants buying for the London market.

Business at Spitalfields is steadily increasing at the expense of Covent Garden. It is now the main market for home-grown fruit and vegetables and many Covent Garden traders have stands at Spitalfields and Spitalfield traders at Covent Garden.

The splendid vehicle parking facilities are a great advantage to Spitalfields, and improvements are constantly developing in all aspects of the marketing of the produce. Time to bring up perishable fruits, such as grapes, from the docks is being cut in every possible way. Fork lift trucks are used in the warehouses. Old-fashioned wooden boxes are being replaced by disposable containers. New methods of grading and packing are often being tried.

Photo: C.O.I.

TEA

THE TEA MARKET

Britain imports more than five and a half thousand million pounds worth of goods and commodities each year. Nearly one third represents food, drink and tobacco. Of this third, more than six per cent represents the value of the tea import.

Even though some tea merchants say rather less tea is consumed these days, because more people are taking to soft drinks or coffee, the British still consume prodigious amounts of tea. Of the two thousand million pounds of tea produced each year, a quarter comes to the United Kingdom. Since a large proportion of it arrives at the Port of London, tea is one of London's most valuable imports, taking value by bulk. Very large quantities also arrive at Bristol and Liverpool.

In 1954, three hundred years after Thomas Garraway first served tea at his coffee house and made it popular, the value of tea arriving at the Port of London, was more than £106,000,000, representing

Photo: B.B.C.

between eighty and eighty-five percent of the nation's tea consumption. In weight this is much the same as before 1939. Bearing in mind that the population has increased by at least six million since then, this accounts for the slightly reduced consumption. But the rate of the decline is now becoming less, which is another way of saying that tea is becoming more popular again. One person consumes an average of $9\frac{1}{2}$ lbs. each year and drinks five and a half cups a day.

61

The price of tea is at least four times what it was before the Second World War, but it is still the cheapest drink available. Nearly two thousand varieties of tea come to London. It arrives from the tea gardens of Northern India, Southern India, Pakistan, Ceylon, Indonesia, Malaya and Vietnam in the East: from Malawi, Kenya, Uganda, Tanzania, West Cameroons, the Congo and Portuguese East Africa in Africa; and from the Argentine and Brazil in South America. The bulk, however, is from Ceylon and India. During 1965, out of 559 million lbs. of tea imported into the United Kingdom, 252 million lbs. were Indian, 176 million lbs. were Ceylon and only 7 million lbs. were China teas.

However, it was in China that tea was first drunk. The earliest records date back to the fourth century A.D. The taste for tea drinking spread to Japan and in the seventeenth century merchants of the Dutch East India Company brought some back as a gift to the Dutch Royal family, from a small Japanese island where China tea was being cultivated.

They liked it, and tea drinking became high fashion amongst the Dutch aristocracy. The Dutch East India Company introduced China tea to England, where it became equally popular amongst the few who could afford it. But as it cost anything up to £10 a lb., it was a rare luxury. The British East India Company, which had been granted its charter in 1600, was the trade rival of the Dutch company and was soon bringing back its own supplies of tea to sell at more reasonable prices. Coffee had already become popular and London saw its first coffee house on Cornhill in 1652. Now advertisements for tea appeared. At Thomas Garraway's coffee house in Exchange Alley, which runs between Cornhill and Lombard Street, appeared this notice:

"Tea in England hath been sold in the leaf for six pounds, and sometimes for ten pounds the pound weight, and in respect of its former scarceness and dearness it hath been only used as a regalia in high treatments and entertainments, and presents made thereof to princes and grandees, till the year 1657. The said Thomas Garraway did purchase a quantity thereof, and first publicly sold the said tea in leaf, a drink made according to the directions of the most knowing merchants and travellers in those eastern countries; and upon knowledge and experience of the said Garraway's continued care and industry in obtaining the best tea, and making drink thereof, very many noblemen, physicians, merchants and gentlemen of quality, have ever since sent to him for the said leaf, and daily resort to his house in Exchange Alley aforesaid to drink the drink thereof . . . These are to give notice that the said Thomas Garraway hath tea to sell from sixteen shillings to fifty shillings a pound."

The following year another advertisement for tea appeared in a London news-sheet. "That excellent and by all Physicians approved China drink called by the Chinese Tcha, by other nations Tay, alias Tee, is sold at the Sultanese Head, a cophee house in Sweeting's Rent, by the Royal Exchange, London."

Like coffee, chocolate and sherbert, tea in the coffee houses was served from barrels. But even at the vastly reduced price of sixteen shillings per pound it was still very expensive. In the wealthy households which could afford it, the tea caddy was always kept locked.

The British East India Company at first imported China and Japanese tea by way of Java. In 1684 the Chinese allowed the company to build a trading station at Canton. After this, tea was brought to England in increasing quantities, but the government now imposed an import duty of 5/- a lb. so that the price remained too high for most people. On the Continent it was selling at less than 1/- a lb. And it was at this period in British history that the smuggler came into his own.

Business men would supply the money, in the first place, for large purchases of tea, tobacco and brandy, which was bought at low prices in Europe. The contraband was brought across the Channel and the North Sea to points off the south and east coasts, where English fishing boats, under cover of darkness, sailed out to meet it. It was transferred to the smacks of the English smugglers and landed secretly along the lonely stretches of shore, where willing hands were waiting to help store it in barns and cellars and even churches. Even the most respectable citizens were subject to temptation where smuggling was concerned. Then, on dark, moonless nights, the night riders set out on the long journey to London, their saddle bags stuffed with illicit packages and kegs. The penalty for smuggling was hanging, but compared with the hundreds who were actually involved, only a relatively small number were caught, which made the risk worthwhile.

It was not until 1784 that the heavy import duties were ended, putting the smugglers out of business, because their dangerous trade was no longer worthwhile. Up to this time, it has been estimated that 7,000,000 lbs. of tea were smuggled into the country each year, compared with the 5,500,000 lbs. which reached it each year by the more orthodox route. And it was during this period that tea became a popular drink of the poor as well as the prosperous.

It was a long haul from China round the Cape of Good Hope to London, for the windjammers of the East India Company were slow and cumbersome. However, they had no competitors until early in the nineteenth century, when American clippers appeared on the China run. They were quicker and lighter and were very soon bringing new season's tea from Canton to London in far less time than the windjammers. So the English began building clippers too, the last survivor being the *Cutty Sark*, which now lies in dry dock at Greenwich, and which you can just see from Machonochie's wool wharf on the Isle of Dogs.

As the signs of rivalry for the China tea trade increased, the East India Company began to consider the possibility of growing tea in India. It was then discovered that the tea tree grew wild in the Assam jungle of North East India.

Experiments in cultivating China tea in India failed, but Charles Bruce, who was acting for the British government, now paid particular attention to the indigenous tea tree of Assam. He transplanted young tea bushes into nursery beds and with the help of Chinese coolies who knew the tricks of the trade—and had been smuggled out of China to help him—Bruce prepared a small sample of Assam tea, which was tasted in Calcutta and approved.

By 1839, ninety-five chests of Assam tea arrived in London and were auctioned. They were liked and the government invited private merchants to take over the Assam tea gardens and produce tea for the British market. People gradually came to prefer Assam tea, which was now treated differently from China tea. The leaves were fermented, producing "black tea." The unfermented tea of China was known as "green tea." By 1850 the Assam company was making a profit. Tea was planted in other parts of India, particularly Darjeeling, in the Himalayan foothills, and the Nilgiri and Anaimalai hills of Madras.

The Indian tea industry grew steadily, and it soon displaced that of China. India became the greatest tea-growing and exporting country in the world. In 1965, India produced 810,000,000 lbs. of tea from seven thousand tea gardens, of which more than half was exported. Tea today is India's most valuable commodity and represents more than twenty per cent of her total exports.

However, within the last few years Ceylon's production of tea has exceeded even that of India's. Up until 1869, Ceylon had been a coffee-growing country. Then came disaster, for a fungus leaf disease attacked and suddenly destroyed all the coffee plantations. The industry received a crippling blow from which it never recovered, and the coffee planters decided to try their fortune with tea. Twenty-five years later, 305,000 acres of tea gardens were flourishing in Ceylon. Today there are 594,000 acres under tea cultivation, and of the 1965 crop of 503,000,000 lbs. of tea, 494,000,000 lbs.—worth about £94 million—were exported, representing sixty-one per cent of Ceylon's entire exports.

In Africa, experiments in tea planting, with Indian seeds and plants, were first carried out, early in the century, in Nyasaland, and then in Kenya, Uganda and Tanganyika. The most recent experiments were conducted in Rhodesia and South Africa.

Compared with India and Ceylon, African production is small, but it is steadily increasing and prospects for the tea industry are good. In some places production has been increased tenfold in the last few years. In 1965, East Africa produced over 100,000,000 lbs. of tea and from Kenya alone the tea exports were worth £6 million.

There are many types of tea, but the basic differences in the varieties on sale in the shops depend more on the treatment of the leaves after they have been plucked than on the type of shrub. The three main classifications of tea are Black tea, Green tea and Oolong tea. Black tea is the kind most people drink in Britain and is the main output of the more important tea-growing countries, such as Ceylon, India, Pakistan and East Africa. It is produced by fermenting the leaves in the course of manufacture. Green tea, which still comes mainly from China and Japan, is not fermented. Oolong tea is semi-fermented. Manufactured in China and Formosa, its export is mainly to the United States of America.

Tea plants can stand a wide range of temperature and are culti-vated as far north as the Russian Caucasus in latitude 45° and as far south as latitude 30° in Natal. However, the best areas are the wet evergreen and warm temperate forest regions. And the most suitable conditions are where the temperature remains mostly between 54° F and 80° F and with at least 60 inches of rain, preferably a good deal more.

In Assam, tea is grown on the flat, alluvial soil of the valley, only a few hundred feet above sea level. Here there is hardly any winter growth and plucking takes place during the hot, wet weather from April to October. In South India and Ceylon, tea is grown from sea level up the mountain slopes, in some places to a height of seven or eight thousand feet, and is cropped all the year round. But on the higher levels the growth of the young leaves is slower. Teas produced in these higher, cooler altitudes are superior in taste and quality to those from the lower slopes, though the yield from each shrub is less.

In East and West Africa, Indonesia, Malaysia and South America, cropping takes place all through the year and the quality varies from the cheap teas growing in the low levels of Portuguese East Africa and Indonesia to the better quality teas from the highlands of Kenya and Tanzania.

If left to grow wild, the tea plant could become a tree up to thirty feet high. But on the tea estates, the plants are carefully pruned so

66

that they form low, spreading shrubs three to four feet high, which can be conveniently plucked by hand.

Tea is made from the young, fresh leaves of the plant, known as the "flush," which are picked every six or seven days. The bulk of the fullgrown, dark green leaves are left on the shrub, to keep the plant in good condition. The newer and tenderer the shoots that are plucked, the better the tea, and it is the tip of the young shoot, "two leaves and a bud," which makes the best tea of all.

The pickers throw the leaves into wicker baskets slung on their backs. Two or three times a day the tea is weighed in the field, for the pickers are paid by the weight of leaves they pluck. The tea is then transported by truck to the estate factory, where the leaves are spread out for some eighteen to twenty-four hours to lose some of their moisture. This process is called "withering" and reduces the leaves to a flabby condition ready for rolling, which is the next process.

The leaves are rolled in a rolling machine to release the juices and during this process they darken and fermentation begins.

After about twenty minutes, the leaves, which by now have massed into twisted lumps, are crushed and sieved. The finer, tenderer leaves come through the sieve and are removed to the fermenting room. The coarser leaves go back for more rolling, until they are in a condition to go through the sieve.

In the humid atmosphere of the fermenting room, the tea is spread into small piles of two to four inches. After two to four hours—depending on the size of the leaf, the temperature and the dampness—the fermentation process will be complete. The tea then goes into a drying machine and is subjected to a current of hot air for about half an hour, when it finally appears as black tea. It is then sieved into the various grades. The finer siftings are known as Dusts, Fannings and Broken Orange Pekoes. The coarser siftings are Orange Pekoes, Pekoes and Broken Pekoes.

This manufactured tea is packed into plywood boxes lined with aluminium foil. All the chests of a particular grade coming from one estate at the same time are known collectively as a "break."

The average break is between thirty and forty chests, each containing about 108 lbs. of tea.

The tea is now ready for marketing. There are several methods, particularly in the case of china tea. A small amount of tea is sometimes sent straight from the tea factories to tea blenders in various parts of the world. Alternatively, tea auctions are held in the countries where it is grown, as, for example, at Calcutta, Cochin in South India, Colombo and Nairobi. The buyers are representatives of international tea companies. These auctions are gaining steadily in importance.

A very large proportion of tea still comes to the United Kingdom to be marketed, however, the three main "tea" ports being Liverpool, Avonmouth and, above all, London. London was once the world market for tea, and a third of the tea sold throughout the world still passes through the auction room at Mincing Lane.

The tea destined for London is usually landed at Tilbury, and lightered up-river to the dockside warehouses around the Pool of London.

The tea is addressed to the brokers in London, who have been engaged by the tea growers to sell it for them. The first task, therefore, of these selling brokers is to visit the warehouse to see whether the cases have arrived in good condition. Having satisfied themselves that they are in order, a hole is bored in the side of a chest from each break and a small quantity of tea extracted. These samples are taken to the tasting rooms. To ease the brokers' work of collecting tea samples from all the different warehouses, the Port of London Authority has established the Tea Sample Distribution Centre in one of their Cutler Street warehouses, where samples from twenty-four London warehouses are brought together.

The selling broker's tea-tasters are able to judge from these samples what the tea from each break is worth and set a tentative figure for the forthcoming auction. The samples are numbered and the catalogues printed.

The buyers also taste the tea, collecting the samples from the Tea Sample Distribution Centre, and they too decide on the price the tea is worth to them. These buyers are the blenders, packers and distributors for the United Kingdom market, many of whom blend, pack and distribute abroad as well.

Brooke Bond and Company, Limited is the largest of these firms of buyers, with over thirty-seven per cent of the home and overseas market. Their huge L-shaped tea-tasting room in Cannon Street is the largest in the world. Here at one time you can see 30,000 samples of different teas. Between twenty-five and thirty different teas go into each blend that is bought in a quarter of a pound package.

As the samples arrive, they are sorted into batches of forty for tasting, each batch containing tea from many different estates. At a first glance, the tasting room looks like a vast and very orderly canteen, with its long tables set with rows of white cups and little teapots and a galaxy of copper kettles steaming on the stove. Look closer and you will see small balances and dishes of tea leaves beside the cups. The tea-tasting procedure is precise and unvarying. 5.65 grams of the tea to be tasted are put into the pot. 280 cubic centimetres of water which has just come to the boil are added and the tea is infused for exactly six minutes by the clock. It is then tipped into a cup containing 5 cubic centimetres of pasteurized milk and the wet tea leaves are tipped into the inverted lid of the pot.

The taster, having examined the dry leaf of the sample for dust and stalk, then notes the size and shade of the leaf. This helps him to decide whether it is suitable for the particular blend he is creating. He then looks at the wet leaves, the shade of which tells him the preserving quality of the tea, and the strength of the tea itself.

Last of all he tastes the tea by sipping a little from a spoon, with a loud, sucking noise, so that it reaches the back of his mouth and the nerves which record both taste and aroma, as well as the taste buds of the tongue. Having tasted the tea, he spits it out into a spittoon.

If, after all this, the taster decides that the tea is suitable for one of his blends, he gives it his own valuation for the benefit of his buying broker, who will bid for him at the auction.

It is by no means easy to keep a popular blend of tea always tasting the same, because tea from the same tea estate may vary in taste at different times of the year. The taste even varies slightly with the time of day at which it is plucked.

Incidentally, tea is apt to take on other tastes if it is carelessly stored in your own home. This is particularly so if the storage place is damp or the tea is kept near a gas stove, or in contact with strong smelling things such as soap, firelighters or highly-scented fruit jellies.

The tea-taster's work is highly skilled and requires years of careful training, so that by the time he has finished testing his samples he has a very good idea of what must be bought at the auction.

Mincing Lane, which runs parallel to Mark Lane, from Fenchurch Street down to Lower Thames Street and the riverside, is one of London's oldest market places, and tea has been auctioned here for more than 130 years. Today the sales are held in the auction room of the Tea Brokers' Association on the top floor of Plantation House.

Sales are held on three days a week, Mondays and Wednesdays being reserved for tea from Northern India, Pakistan, Africa, Indonesia, Japan, Formosa, Mauritius, Malaya, China, Iran and Argentina; and Tuesdays for tea from Ceylon and South India.

The auctioneers act for the growers and their selling brokers, while buying brokers bid for the buyers. The buyers themselves have no wish to disclose to competing firms just which lots they are buying for their exclusive blends. They are usually present at the auctions, however, and have their own methods of contacting their brokers and advising them, if they want to advance the bidding.

A broker acts for several clients, so the fifteen or twenty voices heard bidding represent a very much larger number of buyers. The auctioneer begins at a price near the selling brokers' valuation and bidding usually rises by $\frac{1}{4}$d a lb. The bidding is sharp and quick and as much as 600,000 lbs. of tea can be bought inside an hour. The weekly average of tea sold is estimated at 8,000,000 lbs.

In this great tea market, the bulk of the tea remains in the dockside warehouses. The manufacturing companies pick up the tea from the warehouses and transport it to their own factories and warehouses. The tea blender now sets to work again. Having selected samples of the teas he wants, he makes a sample blend and compares it with the previously distributed blend which he wants to match. If it differs, he tests the individual teas to see where the variation lies. When he is satisfied, the recipe is sent to the factory.

The various teas are brought in from the warehouse and the mixing begins. One of Brooke Bond's large factories is in Aldgate, where the process of the delivery of tea from the dock warehouses, mixing and packaging and dispatching to all parts of the home counties and also abroad goes on continuously, day after day. The despatch room fills up by the end of the day, when it is emptied again, in readiness for the next day's consignments.

When the tea arrives from the docks, the lids of the chests are ripped off, either mechanically or by hand. The tea is tipped onto conveyor belts carrying magnets, to which nails and such extraneous objects conveniently attach themselves. The tea is then screened to remove odd bits of paper and wood. It passes through cutters to trim uneven leaves. An elevator carries the required amounts of the different teas to the top floor of the factory, where they are delivered into one of two blending drums. While one drum is revolving the one next to it is being emptied and filled again, so that there is no pause in the blending operation. After revolving for nine minutes the teas are effectively blended.

The blended tea falls from the drum, through giant hoppers, into one of those tea-packing machines which never fail to intrigue the uninitiated. Yards of muslin are turned into tea bags. Reels of paper and printed card are transformed into neat, lined packages, bearing a coded date mark. The correct amount of tea falls into the package and it is sealed. It takes a minute for the machine to pack a hundred $\frac{1}{4}$ lb. packages, which are then wrapped automatically into 6 lb. parcels and stacked on movable platforms, all ready for loading onto the vans. They are delivered to the docks for export, or to various distribution depots throughout the United Kingdom, from which they are sent out each week to the retailers.

These are the bare bones of the story of tea marketing for the ordinary run of tea drinkers. But the connoisseur can still pay 20/- a lb. for his tea if he chooses. There are no up-to-date figures available for tea production in Russia and China, but the Chinese industry is expanding steadily. If you have a taste for the exotic you can buy either green or black tea from China, delicately scented with gardenia and jasmine flowers.

Photo: Ceylon Tea Centre

WOOL

THE WOOL EXCHANGE

"The wool of Britain is often spun so fine that it is in a manner comparable with the spider's thread."

These words were written by a Roman visiting Britain nearly two thousand years ago. From that time the fame of English wool, from sheep bred on her damp, rich pasturelands, steadily increased. Throughout the Middle Ages, England grew prosperous on the export of her wool to the wool-weaving towns of northern Europe, especially to Bruges and Ghent in Flanders, where the citizens had been engaged in weaving for generations and were extremely skilled.

It was Edward III who encouraged the English weaving industry by inviting Flemish weavers to settle in England and teach their craft to the Englishmen. Some accepted the invitation. Although the outcome was to bring trouble to the Flemish weaving industry, and prosperity to England, there was little the Flemish could do about it, for their business depended on England and the supply of English wool. The

74

Photo: I.W.S.

records are still in existence of one of these Flemish weavers, John Kemp, who came to England to "exercise his art and teach it to such of our people as shall be inclined to learn it." In return, he and his family and work people were given special protection and privileges.

Soon English woollen cloth became as valuable an export as English wool and many cloth-weaving gilds came into existence. The first Flemish weavers settled in East Anglia, but in time they had established weaving towns throughout the Midlands, in the Cotswolds and the Welsh border towns.

By Tudor times, the export of English cloth had become more important than that of raw wool. Records show that in the early fourteenth century England was exporting 30,000 sacks of wool each year and 5,000 bales of cloth. But by the early sixteenth century, the figures had changed to only 4,000 sacks of wool and 100,000 bales of cloth.

All the arts and crafts associated with the production of cloth, such as fulling, stretching and dyeing, developed their own carefully, protected gilds. And, to the discomfiture of the members of the Staple,* who controlled the export of raw wool, the sale of woollen cloth came into the hands of a new company, the Merchant Adventurers.

A great variety of cloths and textiles were produced in England, once the weaving industry was firmly established, with the more delicate techniques learned from the Flemish. But there were as yet no factories, and it remained a cottage industry. The merchants often brought the raw material to the cottage weavers and collected the finished cloth.

About the middle of the sixteenth century there was a slump in the English woollen industry for a time. England had lost Calais. The Netherlands were governed by Spain, and long before war finally broke out between England and Spain, the markets of Antwerp and Bruges were forbidden to the English. England turned to Hamburg as a port of entry to Europe, but it was not long before the German

* Wool collecting centres were called Staples. Every wool merchant had to be a "Member of the Staple."

merchants of the Hanseatic League prohibited the entry of English merchant vessels.

This resulted in unemployment amongst the cottage spinners and weavers, and the creation of the Elizabethan poor laws to relieve the worst sufferers. Before long, however, London merchants planned new markets and English seamen were carrying English woollen fabrics farther afield than Europe—to Russia, Turkey, the Levant, Persia and around the Cape of Good Hope to India.

The wool trade was saved and English merchants and sheep farmers began to prosper once more. The manufacture and export of cloth continued to increase at the expense of the export of raw wool. The Merchant Adventurers gained ground at the expense of the Staplers.

At first the weaving industry had tended to concentrate in York, Coventry, Norwich, Colchester and Salisbury, while London continued to prosper as the main exporting port. However, the actual manufacture was still a cottage industry. A great deal of it took place in the rural areas, so that many villages were partly industrial. In fact, there was a tendency now for skilled cloth manufacturers to move from the towns into the country, perhaps to escape the somewhat overbearing laws of the craft gilds. The important wool merchants developed a system of supplying raw material to village craftsmen owning their own looms and collecting the woven cloth, which was then passed to other craftsmen, usually townsmen, for the finishing processes.

In those days, there was a spinning wheel in nearly every cottage and a weaver's shed in every street. In East Anglia, Coggeshall was nearly as important as Norwich, Colchester and Sudbury, and the industry was as thriving in the Cotswolds and the West.

By the end of the seventeenth century, the import of foreign cloth and raw wool was forbidden. In fact, the government did everything in its power to promote the English woollen industry. It even decreed that the shrouds of the dead should be made of English wool.

The eighteenth century saw the beginnings of the Industrial Revolution. By this time, cotton from America was being spun and woven in Lancashire. Cotton, like wool, was a cottage industry at first. The cotton arrived in increasing quantities at the steadily-growing port of Liverpool, and was spun and woven in the surrounding towns and villages, where the damp climate proved highly suitable for handling it.

Nevertheless, wool was more important than cotton at this time, and the industry was far more widespread. Moreover, the wool trade was still given government protection, for woollen cloth represented nearly half the value of Britain's export trade.

Although the spinning wheel had completely supplanted the hand spindle by the sixteenth century, spinning was a slow business and it took ten spinners to keep a weaver at work. Many experiments were made in an attempt to speed up the process. Richard Arkwright of Bolton devised a machine driven by water power. In 1764 William Hargreaves invented the Spinning Jenny, by which sixteen or more threads could be spun by one spinner at the same time. This was a great step forward and proved particularly suitable for the spinning of wool, the threads of which are not so fine as cotton. In 1774, however, Samuel Crompton, also of Bolton, invented his "mule", which produced an extremely fine thread, suitable for cotton as well as wool. This brought about the beginning of England's industrialization. The mule produced a yarn faster than the weaver could use it, but, within a few years, a fly shuttle had been invented which doubled the weaver's output. Then, in 1785, Cartwright invented his power loom.

Water power was used at first, but experiments now began in steam power. Steam pumps had been used in mining for some years and in 1776 James Watt produced his steam engine. The following year, writing about a new pumping engine he had just installed, he reported that: "The velocity, violence, magnitude and horrible noise of the engine gave universal satisfaction to all beholders."

Machinery meant factories, and the workers moved to the towns where the factories were concentrated. While Manchester became the focus of the cotton industry, the woollen factories were localized in central Yorkshire, around the towns of Bradford and Leeds, between the coal mines of south Yorkshire and the wool supplies of the northern part of the country. By this time the new countries of Australia

78

and New Zealand were developing and sending increasing supplies of wool, so that the English woollen industry grew more important than ever.

The men employed in the more skilled process of weaving did not move to the towns as quickly as the spinners. As late as the beginning of the nineteenth century, despite the steady development of the woollen factories, part of the weaving industry remained domestic and was a source of additional income to many agricultural villages throughout the country. However, once steam power had become fully established, the weavers gradually abandoned their cottage looms, and like the spinners, moved to the big manufacturing towns.

With England's industrialization and the increasing import of wool from Australia and New Zealand, the English countryside changed. Flocks of English sheep dwindled, for it was more profitable to import wool cheaply and manufacture it into woollen cloth. England's industrial expansion during the latter part of the nineteenth century was more rapid than that of any country in the world. She became the largest exporter of manufactured goods, including woollen cloth, but at the same time the greatest importer of food and natural products. Bradford became the "wool" capital of the world and London the world wool market.

Early in the twentieth century, other countries, particularly those of Europe and North America, caught up with Britain in industrialization and strong competitors appeared in the wool industry. However, the world population was increasing, and other markets for Britain appeared in India and the Far East. Britain remained well in the lead. After the First World War came signs of the first real trouble, as India and Japan, paying low wages, began to manufacture textiles in competition with Britain's better quality but more expensive products. During the years following the Second World War, competition quickly increased, particularly from Japan, which now imports a large amount of wool directly from Australia for her woollen industry. America, too, is receiving increasingly large supplies from Australia and New Zealand, which do not pass through London, thereby saving time and freight charges.

However, the British wool textile industry is still the largest in the world and the sixth largest export industry of the United Kingdom. The value of wool exports averages more than £180 million each year.

The main wool-producing countries in the world today are Australia, the Soviet Union, New Zealand, Argentina, South Africa, the United States of America, Uruguay, China and Mongolia, the United Kingdom, Turkey and India. These are the actual production figures for 1964:

Australia	1,794 million lbs.
Soviet Union	760
New Zealand	623
Argentina	419
South Africa	315
United States	265
Uruguay	187
China and Mongolia	170
United Kingdom	128
Turkey	93
India	78

Of this vast supply, Great Britain imports, mainly from Australia, New Zealand and South Africa, over 400 million lbs. each year, more than any other country in the world. This includes the United States, which imports 395 million lbs., and Japan, which imports 350 million lbs. The other three main wool-importing countries are France, consuming 252 million lbs. a year, Italy 190 million and West Germany 148 million.

In the United Kingdom, the main concentration of the wool textile industry is still the West Riding of Yorkshire, with Bradford the most important town, but the Midlands and the West of England have important manufactures. In Scotland, the industry is concentrated in the Central Lowlands and the Border counties.

In 1965 the industry produced 175 million square yards of woollen and 148 million square yards of worsted cloth, 58 million square yards of woven carpets and rugs and 43 million lbs. of knitting wool.

The difference between woollen and worsted cloth is in the yarn. In woollen fabrics the fibres of the yarn lie in all directions, so that the cloth has a slightly fuzzy surface. In worsteds, the yarns used are spun from wool which has been combed. By this process the shorter fibres are removed and the longer ones lie parallel and flat, so that a worsted fabric usually has a smooth surface and you can easily see the weaving structure.

Seventy per cent of British woollen fabrics and ninety-five per cent of the worsteds are made in the West Riding. Scotland and the West of England are renowned for the production of high class woollen cloth. The manufacture of hosiery and knitwear is widely scattered throughout the country. But the two main areas are in Scotland and the east Midlands, while carpets are made in Kidderminster, Halifax, Dewsbury and Durham, in Glasgow and Kilmarnock and several towns in Northern Ireland.

Nearly two thirds of the wool that goes into the carpet manufacture is produced in the United Kingdom, the rest coming from South Africa, New Zealand, South America and the Far East.

Although the United Kingdom is such a large importer of wool it still exports a certain amount of home-grown wool, the percentage in 1964 being 65% of the entire clip.

All this wool is sold through the usual marketing channels.

The wool grown in Australia, New Zealand and South Africa is sometimes auctioned in those countries, much of it being bought by brokers for export. Otherwise it is exported direct and auctioned in the wool markets of the importing countries. United Kingdom wool is marketed by the British Wool Marketing Board and sold by auction in London, Leicester, Bradford, Edinburgh, Exeter and Belfast.

The first public sale of foreign wool took place in London at Mr. Garraway's coffee house in Cornhill, as early as 1821, when 176 lbs. of foreign wool were put up for auction. In 1875, a Wool Exchange was opened in Coleman Street, close to the Guildhall. The first wool auctioned at the Wool Exchange came from Saxony and Spain, but very soon the bulk of its business was in wool from Australia, New Zealand and South Africa, with smaller amounts from Kenya, the Falkland Islands and Chile, and there were also special auctions of English wool.

During the Second World War, there were no wool sales in London, Australia, New Zealand and South Africa. The whole of the wool production of these countries was commandeered by the governments, after valuation. After the war, the stock of 10,000,000 bales was sold by the United Kingdom Wool Disposal Limited, the respective governments receiving their proportionate shares.

London is now trying to recover its earlier importance, but still has a long way to go. Whereas before 1939, an average of 500,000 bales of wool would be sold each year in Coleman Street, in 1958 the figures was down to about 340,000 bales. Moreover, some Bradford manufacturers now buy direct from abroad and large amounts also go direct to Hull and Liverpool. Early in the 1960's, the annual import of wool to London was about £54 million, as compared with £60 million to Hull and £40 million to Liverpool.

However, London is very conveniently placed for European buyers, and wool bought in London can be delivered quickly, which is particularly useful for the "spot" market, when manufacturers need a relatively small additional supply of one particular kind of wool to complete a contract.

In 1962, the Exchange in Coleman Street was demolished for a redevelopment plan and the Wool Exchange moved to Spitalfields, where the magnificent Fruit Exchange had been built in 1929.

The Fruit Brokers leased one of their large auction rooms to the London Wool Brokers, a fourth floor for additional offices was added, and the building was renamed the London Fruit Exchange and London Wool Exchange.

Following the Second World War and up till 1959, the wool auctions in London were run by the Committee of London Wool Brokers, who represented the six firms of brokers engaged in selling wool. Now they are run by a private company, London Wool Brokers, Ltd.

The wool, already classified and graded, arrives at the London docks in huge bales, each weighing three hundredweights and bearing the mark of the grower. When these bales are loaded onto the ships, they are compressed with giant presses to half their original size, in order to save shipping space.

From the docks, they are lightered up to the dockside wool warehouses.

The warehouse of the London Wool Brokers is at Machonochie's Wharf. This is a private wharf on the Isle of Dogs—that strange peninsula of land, so busy yet at times so desolate looking—which is created by the U-shaped bend of the Thames flowing southward along Limehouse Reach, eastward through the Greenwich Reach and north again along the Blackwall Reach, before curving northeastward again in to Bugsby's Reach.

Machonochie's Wharf is surrounded by the great complex of the West India docks and on this stretch of the river, with a glimpse of the Greenwich Observatory on the opposite bank away to the east, the quiet, purposeful lighters are constantly at work. In these days of automation, it is refreshing to see a small lighter nose its way gently and efficiently to the side of the wool wharf and watch the cranes unloading. There is still the faintly rural atmosphere of a country barn about the warehouse, with its steep, wooden, ladderlike steps and the countless bales of wool.

Wool is one of the commodities which is bought from samples. Up on the first floor is the huge sample room, with a glass roof admitting the necessary north light, so that the buyers who come to inspect the wool can make a proper examination.

A small cut is made in each bale of wool, or from one of a collection of similar bales, and samples of about three pounds are extracted. These samples are placed in cellophane bags, carefully numbered, and arranged in wire trays on long tables. The sample room looks like the hall of a museum, the more so since the trays are protected by black, cellophane covers, to prevent the wool from fading.

The selling brokers first examine these samples, make their valuations and inform the agents of the owners. The reserve prices for the auction are fixed and the catalogues are then printed, giving a description of the type of wool and the marks and numbers of the bales.

A day or two before the sale, buyers come to make their examination and selection, marking their catalogues with the lots for which they intend to bid. These men, wearing traditional white coats, are extremely knowledgeable and from the "handle" and appearance of the wool can tell the type, breed and origin of the sheep.

The wool auction room at Spitalfields is one of the largest auction rooms in the country and can accommodate about five hundred buyers. To this oak-panelled amphitheatre, with its tiers of seats, come buyers from Bradford and the north of England as well as manufacturers' representatives from European countries, particularly France and Holland. Bidding is brisk and noisy, prices advancing at $\frac{1}{4}$d a lb. until the price reaches 75d. a lb. and after that in advances of $\frac{1}{2}$d a lb. Though the buyers are quick, the auctioneer is always in complete control. He sits unperturbed by the yapping and yelping, as the buyers excitedly make their bids. Two assistants, sitting on either side of the auctioneer, make a careful note of the bids. Lot by lot, he offers the wool which the clients of his company wish to sell, and an average of 2500 bales can be sold in a two-hour session.

There have been very sharp fluctuations in the price of wool during the last fifteen years and manufacturers have devised a method of protecting themselves from heavy losses if they have bought large stocks at a high cost and the price slumps. This works in a similar way to the "Futures" market in corn at the Baltic Exchange.

Raw wool is of variable quality, however, and, at first, merchants had to establish a certain standard, which would serve as a basis for buying and selling. They decided that a partly processed form of wool would be better than raw wool, and chose a sliver of combed wool, which is prepared for the first stage of spinning. This is known as a wool "top".

The "Futures" market in wool tops is run by the London Wool Terminal Market Association at Plantation House in Mincing Lane, and is available to merchants who want to protect themselves against risk of loss through fluctuating prices. As at the Baltic, prices are

84

called across the "ring" and marked on a board. The assumption is that the fluctuation in the price of the tops will follow the same course as that of raw wool. Only members are allowed to enter the floor and bid across the ring. The chairman announces the opening of business and it continues for five minutes, the members bidding across the ring. Then they bargain amongst themselves. A merchant or his broker buys at the current London price, so that he can sell again at a profit if the value of the wool he is shipping from Australia drops before it reaches London, or cover his losses on the Futures market if the price rises.

A buyer on this market must pay up within eighteen months. But more often than not he sells again, and it is rare for him to receive the wool tops he has bought on paper for his own manufacture.

This market is in no way connected with the Wool Exchange, where the wool is actually sold for immediate delivery, but it is an ingenious protective or "hedging" device which is used by many merchants buying on the Wool Exchange.

Apart from competition from foreign woollen manufacturers, the British woollen industry is also suffering from the increasing use of synthetic fibres, particularly in the manufacture of carpets. This means that the consumption of wool in Britain is declining. In 1959 it was 518 million lbs., but by 1964 it was down to 418 million lbs., while the output of synthetic fibres from mineral and vegetable sources, such as nylon, Terylene, Courtelle and Acrilan, has been expanding rapidly.

British textile manufacturers have developed a number of methods of blending man-made fibres with natural fibres and with each other, producing fabrics with new textures and hues, which are moisture-absorbent, hard-wearing, light, warm and have drip-dry and non-creasing properties. The export of these both as yarn and manufactured fabrics now amounts to more than £58 million a year. And despite the cry of the Wool Secretariat that "You can't fake the real thing" the man-made fibre industry strives strenuously to prove that you can.

In 1964, British carpet manufacturers made £146 million worth of carpets and rugs, of which £10.6 million were exported, Australia being the largest market. Almost half of these were the Axminister type of carpet and about a third contained a high proportion of artificial fibres mixed with the wool. More than half contained considerably more man-made fibre than wool.

Buyers inspecting the wool before sale at London Docks   Photo: I.W.S.

FURS

THE FUR MARKET

From earliest times, mankind has traded in furs. It is an odd fact that though Great Britain is so far from the great fur-producing countries of the world, being about halfway between the northern, fur-breeding regions of Canada and those of Europe and Asia, the London fur market is the most important in the world. Moreover, it is still in the small, historic area, close to the river, where the City of London's trade in furs began, at least two thousand years ago.

There is no open market for furs, where members of the public can see the skins on display, But if you make your way from St. Paul's Cathedral toward the Thames, across Cannon Street and Queen Victoria Street, you will come upon the "fur quarter" of the City. On College Hill, Queen Street, Garlick Hill and all the other narrow lanes which run down steeply from Queen Victoria Street to the western end of Upper Thames Street, there are a number of fur ware-houses and the offices of fur-trading companies and fur-brokers of all

Photo: Radio Times

descriptions. On Garlick Hill stands Beaver House, which houses the London headquarters of the Hudson's Bay Company. It was opened in 1928 and is an elegant, modern building, almost opposite the little church of St. James, Garlickshythe, which Christopher Wren built after the original, medieval church was destroyed during the fire of London.

In the Strathcona Room of Beaver House is the London Fur Exchange, where fur dealers meet to exchange news and discuss business. But the actual dealing in furs takes place during the great fur auctions which are held at Beaver House four times a year, in the spring, summer, autumn and winter, each lasting for from four to six weeks. There are also important special auctions from time to time, for the sale of certain skins such as mink and Persian lamb.

There are three large firms of furbrokers or auctioneers in London, all of them having their headquarters in the "fur quarter" of the city. The broker is the middleman who represents the fur producer and sells to the merchant firms who require the skins. Each of the three brokers specializes in the handling of the furs from a particular part of the world. The Hudson's Bay Company, the largest of the three, specializes chiefly in furs from Canada.

Furs arrive at the London warehouses in this corner of the City from all over the world. Sable, marten, mink, ermine, red and silver fox, lynx, wolf, beaver, musquash (muskrat), otter, bear and squirrel come from Canada and Siberia and the white fox and seal from even farther north, within the Arctic Circle. Skunk, raccoon and oppossum come from the United States; oppossum, wallaby and hundreds of rabbit skins from Australia; astrakhan, caracul and tiger, sheep and goat skins from Central Asia, and the rare chinchilla from Peru and Argentina.

Nowadays many fur-bearing animals are bred in captivity. There are fur-ranches in America, Canada and Scandinavia for mink, chinchilla and foxes; in South West Africa for Persian lamb and in Britain for mink and chinchilla. This method of producing fur is steadily increasing. Nevertheless, a great many animals are still trapped and the fur-trapper's life is a very hard one. In Canada,

around the more southerly shores of Hudson's Bay, the work is done
by Indians, but farther north, above about latitude 55° N, the trap-
pers are Eskimos.

An animal's fur is at its best in the winter and, as the snow and ice
close in, the Indian trapper sets out with his sledge and team of dogs
on his long, solitary trek. This may take him anything up to two
thousand miles away from his home, and can last for eight or nine
months. He carries little food for himself and his dogs, for he hunts
most of it during his travels. His equipment is only a blanket, a small
tent, pemmican—which is dried meat—bacon, flour, tea, tobacco, an
axe, matches, firearms and ammunition, traps and reindeer thong.

When he reaches his hunting ground, he makes camp and acquires
a supply of food. Then he sets out on a fifty-mile circuit, setting his
traps in places where long experience has taught him that he is most
likely to be successful. When he has made his round trip and reached
his camp again it is time to examine his first trap. For the next three
or four days, taking with him only his blankets, a minimum of food
and his gun, he makes the round of the traps. When he finds a
trapped animal, he shoots and skins it on the spot and packs the fur
onto his sledge. When he has collected a good supply of skins, he
makes his way to the nearest trading post. Here he sells the skins,
sometimes for money, sometimes in exchange for food, clothing and
any other things he may want.

Then off he sets again on another hunting trip in a different area,
and the whole process is repeated. From the trading posts the skins
are carried over the snow and ice and frozen rivers to the nearest
railroad. From there the furs are despatched to the Canadian warehouses for export to London.

The Eskimo fur hunters obtain a large proportion of their furs from
the sea—from seals, fur seals and a few sea otters. The fat from these
animals provides the Eskimos with much of their food and other
necessities of life. This includes even lighting and heating, nearly all
of which is derived from melted "blubber", which is animal fat.

When the skins reach the London warehouses they are sorted and
graded. A great deal of skill and knowledge is needed for this work,

and the London graders are famous for their reliability. There are, for example, sixty-four recognizable grades into which the skins of Persian lamb are graded, though to the inexperienced eye all the skins look very much alike.

The graded skins are made up into bundles of usually two hundred skins. If there are several bundles of similar quality, they are grouped together as a "string".

Once this work is finished, a catalogue is prepared for the auction, listing the type of skin, the number of skins in the bundle, the letter and number which will indicate to the experienced fur buyer the type, grade and district from which the skin comes.

There is not enough room to display all the skins to the buyers, nor the time to examine them. Enormous numbers of skins are sold at these auctions, so a few days before the sale sample bundles of skins are set out in the warehouse display rooms. The grading is so skilful that the buyers can be confident that the sample shown is an absolutely fair example of the bulk of the lot it represents.

Buyers come from all over the world to inspect the samples of skins. Piles of stiff beaver skins are arranged with the fur side downward so that they look to all the world like a collection of small Zulu shields. Neat clusters of beautiful mink are strung together and laid out on wide trays set on benches. Endless rows of silver, blue and red foxes, all on rails, under a strong north light, are deftly arranged by the white-coated warehousemen.

When the buyers have made a thorough examination of the samples, they mark their catalogues with the lots for which they want to bid, and await the day of the sale.

The buying is done by both London and international dealers, who buy on commission for British manufacturers or overseas buyers, though some merchants buy directly at the auctions in order to re-sell. However, only authorized fur dealers may bid. One of the conditions of the sales is that "prospective purchasers must produce to the company during the week prior to the auction evidence satisfactory to the company of their qualification to purchase."

The skins are still in the raw state when they are auctioned and are rather stiff. Many skins are re-exported, still in this raw state, a large number going back to Canada, their country of origin. Sometimes, however, skins are dressed before being re-exported. Others are dressed and dyed.

In and around London there are a number of factories engaged in this work. During the last few years, as a result of careful experiments in the factory laboratories, important advances in techniques have been made.

The processing of seal skins has been a speciality of London craftsmen for over a century. Special consignments of seals are sent regularly to London for processing from the Pribiloff Islands in the Bering Sea, from off the Cape of Good Hope in South Africa, as well as from Newfoundland and Norway. The finished skins are re-exported to fur markets all over the world. Within the last thirty years, British furriers have also specialized in the processing and dyeing of beaver, nutria, mole, Persian lamb, musquash and marmot furs and their unique skill is highly valued in foreign markets.

Making a fur coat needs similar delicate and experienced craftsmanship. The designer first makes a canvas shape from which a paper pattern is cut. Then the sorter takes over, selecting skins which match as nearly as possible. A mink coat, for example, will take anything from seventy-five to a hundred skins, so matching is obviously extremely important. The cutter then cuts his skins to fit the shape of the coat and the machinist sews them together.

While the coat is still in flat pieces, the parts are damped and nailed out over the pattern. Then they are dried and softened in revolving drums before being finally sewn together into a finished coat and lined.

These manufactured coats are also exported, but an increasingly important aspect of the exporting business is the making of what are called "shells and plates". These are sets of skins sewn together into oblong pieces, sufficient to make a fur coat. These sets are increasingly in demand for export and together with the raw skins, processed and dyed skins and fully made coats form an important item of Britain's exports, amounting to something like £25,000,000 a year.

The fur auctions all take place in Beaver Hall, the large auction room at Beaver House, which is approached by the entrance in Garlick Hill. It is like a large lecture theatre, with tiers of green, leather-covered seats facing a platform on which sit the auctioneer with three spotters on either side of him. It is the job of the spotters to watch the bidding and make sure that none escapes notice, for the bidders sit in silence and indicate their bids only by signs.

There is little in the decorous atmosphere of the room to indicate all the hard work which goes into the fur trade, from the lonely, arctic trek of the trapper to the workroom of some exclusive furrier house, where the final label is sewn inside a luxurious fur coat. The number of the lot for sale appears in a lighted sign above the auctioneer and he calls out the rising prices as each bidder's signal is spotted by himself and his colleagues.

Bidding, though silent, is brisk. It is a tradition that the sale always begins with the furs of the Hudson's Bay Company. Of these, beaver—which was its first merchandise—comes first.

In the first day's sale of the 1967 spring auction 15,000 beaver skins were sold in 199 lots, 186,000 musquash, 2720 otter skins, nearly 80,000 ermines, 65,000 squirrels, almost 3,000 martens, 2,600 wild minks and 60,000 silver, blue and red foxes. The prices made at Beaver Hall affect fur prices in every other fur market in the world.

The market is, of course, subject to changes in fashion. During the 1930's, silver foxes were popular. Then they lost popularity and mink and Persian lamb became the rage. For many years the silver foxes hung unwanted in the warehouses, but now, though mink and Persian lamb are still high fashion, the silver fox is coming into its own again.

During the war, the fur market of London was closed and the international trade moved to New York. In the 1950's, however, the London fur trade, with its traditional skills, gradually re-established itself. Despite strong competition from America as well as the large fur markets of Europe—particularly in Russia and Germany—it has reached its old importance again and still holds its own as the principal fur market of the world.

The story of how this came about in the first place goes back many hundreds of years. Fur has always been highly valued. When the Romans arrived in Britain they traded furs for British wool and metals. With the passing centuries, after the Roman Empire collapsed and the Romans left Britain and their beautiful city of London, the English arrived, and it was King Alfred who rebuilt the quays of London. His trading ships were anchored in the Thames in midstream and the cargoes were rowed ashore in barges to the docks at Billingsgate and Queenhythe, which in time were to be connected by Lower and Upper Thames Street.

Norse traders brought many exotic luxuries to Queenhythe, including furs from Russia and Armenia. The Anglo-Saxons wore furs, but it was amongst the Normans that they became particularly popular. During the Middle Ages German and Flemish traders, who belonged to the great trading organization known as the Hanseatic League, settled in the Steel Yard, which lay between Upper Thames Street and the shores of the river. The League traded in many things, including furs, and it was at the Steel Yard that they established their main fur market.

Before this time, only the members of the Court and the nobility could afford to wear furs. Their cloaks were lined with furs and men's tunics and women's dresses were trimmed with sable and ermine. However, as England grew rich with her export of wool, many merchants and their wives took to wearing furs. The Company of Skinners was one of the earliest of the medieval gilds and it grew very rich and prosperous during these years, drawing up regulations for the importing and manufacturing of skins into furs.

During the reign of Edward III, in the fourteenth century, a law was passed decreeing that only members of the Court and the nobility might wear ermine and sable, and the wives of tradesmen must wear the furs of "lambs, rabbits, cats and foxes". This may have been because of a fear that the rarer, fur-bearing animals were being overtrapped and threatened with extinction or a rather desperate measure to try and keep the rising middle classes in their place. Whatever the reason, it was a setback to the foreign fur trade for many years to come. But in the early seventeenth century, its fortunes revived as men took to wearing large felt hats made from beaver fur, which was first brought to Europe by French cod-fishermen from the gulf of the St. Lawrence river.

These were the years of the great journeys of discovery by both land and sea. Henry VII had sent John Cabot's expedition to the New World at the end of the fifteenth century. But it was not till early in the seventeenth century that an Englishman, Henry Hudson, followed him across the Atlantic to explore the river and the shores of the great bay which were to be named after him. Hudson returned to England with stories of the vast numbers of wild animals around the shores of Hudson Bay, with pelts which would produce a great wealth in furs. He returned to North America but died in an attempt to find the northwest passage to Asia.

The French had already established colonies along the St. Lawrence river, and were exploring south and west into the heart of North America. A French traveller, Pierre Radisson, turned north and reached the shores of Hudson Bay, where he began a flourishing fur trade, but the French government intervened, declaring that he was trading without a licence. They confiscated most of his furs, whereupon Pierre Radisson left Canada, and after a consultation with the English commissioner in Boston, arrived in London. He obtained an audience with Charles II and outlined to him a plan for developing the fur trade in Canada.

The King was interested and an expedition was organized. The King, his brother the Duke of York—who was later to become James II—his cousin, Prince Rupert, and many important London merchants all contributed to the cost of the expedition. Two vessels set sail from Gravesend, of which one had to turn back after running into bad weather, but the *Nonesuch* reached Hudson Bay safely and remained there for seven months. She returned to London with a cargo of furs which were so valuable that the excited merchants persuaded the King to grant a royal charter to a new fur-trading company.

Prince Rupert was the first governor of the company, which was given powers to operate the vast territory comprising all the rivers which drain into Hudson Bay. It was called the Company of Adventurers of England trading into Hudson Bay.

The first company meetings were held in Prince Rupert's private quarters in the Tower of London, and they soon found that they had so many furs that they hardly knew how to dispose of them. Some were sold privately. Others were sent to the fur dealers of Leipzig, Amsterdam, Paris and Vienna. But the quality and quantity of the furs reaching London was so high that the European dealers were soon coming to London to buy.

Coffee houses had recently been opened in London, where merchants met to do business. The proprietors provided not only food and drink and newspapers but often a saleroom where commodities could be auctioned. It was at Mr. Garraway's coffee house in Change Alley off Cornhill that the first London fur auction took place, in December, 1671. Mr. Garraway announced that "3,000 weight of Beaver Skins, comprised in thirty lotts, will be offered for sale."

Bidding was "by candle". In place of a bell, which was later to be the signal for bids to be offered, the auctioneer lit an inch of candle and bidding continued until the candle had burned itself out and the flame died.

The business of the Hudson's Bay Fur Company steadily increased. Apart from all the other furs they had to offer, they held the monopoly of beaver, and men continued to wear beaver hats for many years to come, until they were outmoded early in the nineteenth century, about the time of Waterloo, by the newly-invented tall silk hat.

In the early years there was strong opposition from the French fur-trading companies in Canada. But by the end of the Seven Years War, in 1763, French territories in Canada were ceded to Britain. By virtue of the vast, fur-bearing territories which had now become part of the British Empire, the Hudson's Bay Company's fur market in London remained the world headquarters of the trade.

The Company outgrew Garraway's and moved to a saleroom in Fenchurch Street, where it remained until 1865. By this time, the population of Canada had greatly increased. The Hudson's Bay

Company still had the power to administrate the regions allotted to it in the seventeenth century, which represented almost two-thirds of the whole country. This arrangement had become both impractical and unjust and, in 1857, the company surrendered its land rights though still retaining its right to trade.

The company moved to the old silk warehouse of the East India Company in Wine Street for some years and then, in 1928, to Beaver House, which also became the headquarters of the entire London fur trade. The London Fur Exchange was opened there in 1933.

Today, the Hudson's Bay Fur Company remains the largest organization in the trade, and although most of its activities are in Canada, the headquarters are still in London. A most important trade organization is the British Fur Trade Association, whose offices are in Upper Thames Street, close to ancient Queenhythe, where the first foreign furs were landed in Anglo-Saxon times, and only a short distance from the beautiful hall of the Worshipful Company of Skinners on Dowgate Hill.

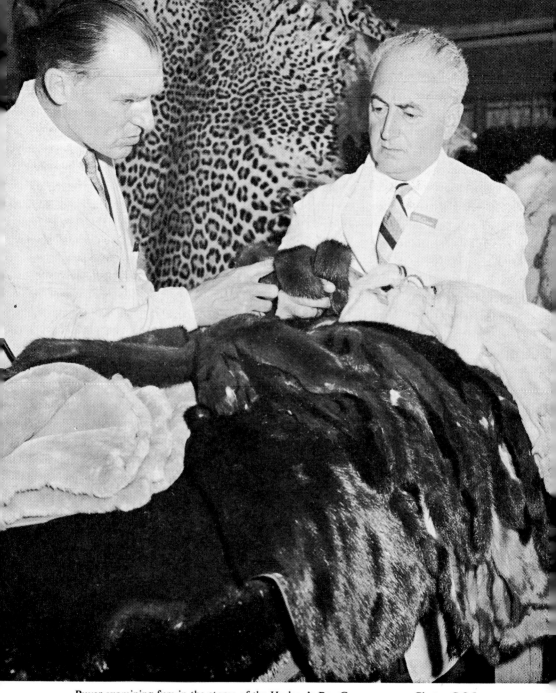

Buyer examining furs in the stores of the Hudson's Bay Company   Photo: C.O.I.

METALS

THE LONDON METAL EXCHANGE

The early civilizations of mankind were based on the discovery and use of metals. The first metal to become known to men of the Stone Age was copper. Then they discovered tin and mixed it with copper, to make the more useful alloy of bronze, which they fashioned into weapons and tools, as well as jewellery. The Phoenicians were visiting Britain to trade for Cornish tin three thousand years ago. But it was probably not until a thousand years later that iron was discovered and used in the Eastern Mediterranean. The Celts, who had mastered the art of forging iron, did not arrive in Britain until about 450 B.C.

After that time, metals did not receive much attention in the history books, particularly the four base metals, copper, tin, lead and zinc, which today are traded on the London Metal Exchange.

In medieval times, tin was mined in Cornwall and lead in Derby-shire, the Mendip Hills and in Devon. In 1182 Richard I granted the

Bidding at the Metal Exchange   Dunbar Economics

Bishop of Bath all the lead on his Somersetshire estates, and, nearly fifty years later, Henry II granted a succeeding Bishop the right to mine lead and iron in the royal forest of Mendip. These concessions were very valuable, for lead was in great demand by the builders for drainage pipes and it was also beginning to be used for roofing. Leaden Hall, as we read in Chapter Three, had a remarkable lead roof, which gave the house its name.

English metal workers were very skilled and at this time were making beautiful leaden fonts for the churches. Pewter, which is an alloy of lead and silver, was also used a great deal. English pewter work was far-famed, and a valuable export to the Continent, as well as being in great demand at home for platters and drinking vessels.

By Tudor times, mining had become an important industry in England. Men often worked in the fields during the summer months and mined below the fields during the winter, under the direction of the steward of the estate on which they were employed. But in some places mining had become full-time work. The tin mines of Devon and Cornwall and the lead mines of Somerset and Derbyshire operated on a full-time basis and, by the end of the seventeenth century, the copper mines of Cornwall were in production.

In England as late as the eighteenth century, the chief use for copper, apart from coins, was for pans and kettles, while lead was still used for pipes and roofing, and also to make shot. With the development of the china and porcelain industries, which were now turning out increasing quantities of tableware and cups and saucers, as well as china teapots for the new and popular drink of tea, pewter was going out of fashion. This meant that there was little demand for tin. As yet zinc was hardly used, except for mixing with copper to make brass.

However, Britain's rapid industrialization during the nineteenth century, with its new machinery and new techniques, created a sudden demand for copper, tin, lead and zinc in ever-increasing quantities.

At the beginning of the nineteenth century, Great Britain was the leader in the world metal trade. Most of the tin and copper in the world came from Cornwall and large quantities of lead were mined in the Pennines. The other great metal-producing regions of the world were as yet undeveloped.

To meet the increasing demand for copper, production was increased in Cornwall, but other countries also began to develop their resources, so that by 1900 the United States was the main world producer, followed by Spain, Chile, Australia and the United Kingdom. Since then, the vast resources of Central Africa have been mined.

Malaya was the leading producer of tin, followed by the Dutch

East Indies, the United Kingdom, Australia and Bolivia. Today there is a world shortage of tin and the production of the Cornish tin mines is being increased again.

In regard to lead, the United States of America had become the largest producer, followed by Spain, Germany, Mexico, Australia and the United Kingdom.

Germany produced the most zinc, followed by Belgium, the United States of America, France and the United Kingdom.

Great Britain was able to export metals for the first part of the nineteenth century, but as her own manufactures absorbed more and more metals there came a time when she had none to spare for export. Then she had to begin importing and, before long, became the largest importer in the world. Much of the overseas mining developments had been promoted with British money, so it is not surprising that London became the general clearing house and exchange for the world's surpluses of metals.

In the uncertain days of sail, the importation of metals into the United Kingdom was inevitably at irregular intervals. This meant that there were wide variations of price. Sometimes the metals were in short supply and urgently needed, but there were periods when there was a surplus which had to be stored. The Metal Exchange was eventually created to solve these problems, and regulate the supply of metals to the manufacturers at relatively stable prices.

Merchants and their brokers began to meet at the Jerusalem Coffee house in Cowper Street off Cornhill. Here they were able to acquire from each other information about the amounts of metal which were being moved across the world, and also the amounts which manufacturers were needing. By the 1850's, the metal dealers had taken to meeting each day at the Royal Exchange, to do business in the buying and selling of copper, lead and tin. But the actual metals were rarely seen, except by the "assayers", who visited warehouses and ports to inspect the metals and certify that the weights and quality were correct.

At the end of the 1860's, the metal dealers were meeting on the ground floor of the newly-opened Lombard Exchange. By 1877, business had grown to such large proportions that a small group of leading metal dealers formed the London Metal Exchange Company, which they organized along similar lines to the Baltic and other Commodity Exchanges.

In 1882, the Exchange moved to the small, simple building which it still occupies. It is in Whittington Avenue, hidden away off Leadenhall Street and adjoining the market. The history of the site goes back many centuries before medieval Leaden Hall as the Exchange is on the site of the Forum of Roman London. The building was reconstructed in 1961 but it still retains its air of quiet Victorian dignity and prosperity. Inside is an atmosphere of friendly, purposeful decorum, created by men with keen, perceptive minds, capable of making quick decisions of world-wide significance, for the Exchange is now the largest metal market in the world for copper, tin, lead and zinc. More than £500 million of business is transacted here each year and the amount is steadily increasing. About thirty per cent of this business is for the home market, the remaining seventy per cent for markets abroad.

The daily prices of metal throughout the world vary with the amounts which each country buys and sells on that particular day. As a large proportion of these sales take place on the London Exchange, the prices which the Exchange publishes each day are recognized as a fair reflection of current world prices.

The Exchange gives its members opportunities to buy at current prices for immediate delivery and also for delivery three months ahead, at the price which "futures" deliveries happen to be commanding. This "hedging" device is similar to that used on the Baltic Exchange and also in the Wool Tops market and other Futures Markets at the London Commodity Exchange.

Let us suppose that a merchant has agreed to supply a customer with a hundred tons of Australian lead. The customer has agreed to buy it at the price it will be when it reaches London a month later. The merchant pays £80 a ton for it to the Australian mining company, but by the time it reaches London the market price has fallen to £78 a ton. This is the price at which he has agreed to supply his customer, so he loses £200 on the deal, at £2 a ton. Since, however, the merchant is a member of the London Metal Exchange, he can avoid this loss by negotiating a "hedge" transaction on the Exchange.

As soon as he has placed his order in Australia for 100 tons of lead at £80 a ton he sells on the London Metal Exchange, as a hedge, 100 tons of lead for delivery in a month's time, at £80 a ton. When the lead from Australia is sold to his customer in London at £78 a ton, he then buys in on the Exchange 100 tons of lead at £78 a ton, in order to fulfil his earlier London Metal Exchange hedge sale. The merchant has now really completed two transactions: he has purchased in Australia lead at £80 a ton and sold it direct to his customer in London at £78 a ton, and also sold forward 100 tons on the Exchange at £80 a ton and bought from the Exchange at £78 a ton. Although he has sustained a loss of £200 on his first transaction, this is offset by a £200 profit on the second transaction.

This "hedging" device is as good as an insurance policy to the dealer and helps to keep the manufacturers' prices stable.

The third function of the Exchange is as a physical market, where metals can be bought and sold at any time.

In 1966 the amounts of metals traded on the Exchange were:

1,282,975 tons of copper
87,695 tons of tin
438,775 tons of lead
303,475 tons of zinc

and the stocks of metals in the registered warehouses of the Exchange at the end of 1966 were:

Copper	14,100 tons
Tin	1,275 tons
Lead	9,438 tons
Zinc	2,834 tons

The market is composed of about forty metal firms, who are known as "Ring" members, and business must be conducted only through one of these firms.

Dealings in copper, lead and zinc are in minimum quantities of twenty-five tons and in tin the minimum quantity is five tons. The metals are prepared in bars, ingots, slabs or plates of standard sizes and weights, so that the purchaser knows exactly what he is buying, without having to view it first.

Marketing for both immediate delivery and for the "futures" takes place at the same time. Business is on five days a week and begins at noon. The Ring members assemble in the large Exchange room and take their seats, their clerks and clients gathering around. The members sit literally in a ring, which consists of four, curved, leather-upholstered benches, each with ten seats, facing inward to form a complete circle. The secretary of the Exchange presides on a small rostrum overlooking the members.

At exactly 12 o'clock, a bell rings and an electric sign indicates COPPER. For the next five minutes the Ring members make bids and offers for copper, calling the prices and acceptances across the Ring. The sales are recorded by their clerks and at the end of the allotted time the bell rings again and dealings in copper cease. TIN appears on the indicator and five minutes are devoted to tin deals. 12.10 to 12.15 is for lead and 12.15 to 12.20 for zinc.

After a ten-minute interval the whole process is repeated and the morning's business ends at 12.55 p.m. The afternoon business is similar, beginning at 3.45 p.m. and ending at 4.35 p.m.

As an international market registering world prices in metals, as they fluctuate with supply and demand, the London Metal Exchange does invaluable work, and its scope is increasing. The Exchange has recently established delivery points for metals in Hamburg, Antwerp and Rotterdam, so that the metals bought in London can be shipped directly to any of these cities from their country of origin, without passing through London at all. The Exchange is also planning to establish markets in aluminium, mercury, wolfram and silver.

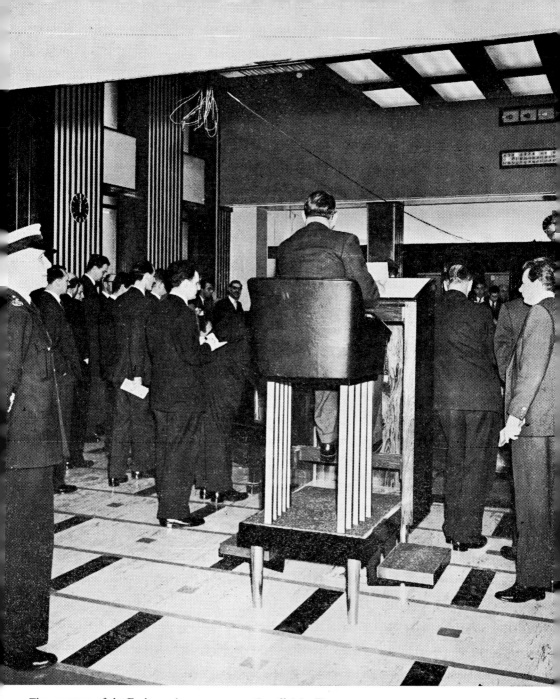

The secretary of the Exchange keeps an eye on the official selling.

Photo: Sport and General Press Agency

GRAIN

THE CORN EXCHANGE

The three main British corn crops are wheat, barley and oats. Wheat flour is the chief constituent of bread—and bread, as we all know, is the staff of life. We may despise it because it is something which is nearly always around in our homes. Some may condemn it because it is said to be fattening. Nevertheless, it is a basic food and perhaps only at times when there is a threatened shortage of bread do we stop to think how much we should miss it if it became unobtainable. Wheat flour also goes into the making of biscuits, cakes and puddings.

Today Great Britain produces nearly half the wheat flour she consumes. The actual figure is 47% but before the 1939 war it was down to 23%. The rest of her wheat supplies have to be imported. In fact, Great Britain imports more wheat than any other country in the world.

Flour from English wheat is too soft to make bread to suit modern tastes and has to be mixed with wheat from such countries as Austra-

British Sugar Corporation

lia, Argentina and Canada, which have much more sunshine and far less rain. However, English wheat, grown in her cool, wet climate, is excellent for making biscuits, as it produces a soft, doughy flour. This is why English biscuits are considered to be the best in the world.

Barley is the most valuable British corn crop today, and she now grows all she needs. About a tenth of this crop—some 1,000,000 tons

—is bought by the brewers for malting. The rest is used by the manufacturers of animal feeding stuffs which, in these days of intensive
production, is an industry of rapidly growing importance. To feed
her large herds of cattle, her flocks of sheep, her pigs and poultry,
British manufacturers import ingredients such as linseed cake, cotton
seed cake, ground nuts and oil and mix them with her home-grown
barley.

Oats are grown far less than in the old days and the trade is
declining, for the simple reason that there are so few horses left in the
country to be fed. Oats today are grown mainly for porridge and
breakfast foods.

The actual figures for the growth of these cereals in Britain today,
compared with the pre-war figures, are interesting. During the 1930's,
there were 48,475,000 acres of land under cultivation in the United
Kingdom and the latest present day figures give a slight increase to
48,614,000 acres. Of this, 1,856,000 acres were under wheat in 1939
compared with an increase to 2,206,000 today, 929,000 acres of
barley in 1939 compared with the enormous increase to 5,032,000
today and 2,403,000 acres of oats which has now dropped to 1,125,000
acres, considerably less than half.

The crops produced in Britain today amount to 3,639,000 tons of
wheat, 7,398,000 tons of barley and 1,326,000 tons of oats.

All this produce has to be marketed. Many country towns have
their own corn markets for the buying and selling of relatively small
amounts of cereals, for local millers and small farmers. But the
selling of home-grown corn in bulk, that is, in amounts of over about
fifty tons, is handled through the larger Corn Exchanges.

The main business of importing wheat and other related products is
handled through London's Baltic Exchange. This organization had
its origins in the seventeenth century, at the time when Britain began
to need foreign wheat in addition to her own supplies. But the Corn
Exchange has a longer history.

Before Britain became industrialized she grew all her own cereals,
though even during the Middle Ages, after an exceptionally poor
harvest, she sometimes imported grain from the Baltic countries. In

those days, and for many years to come, the staple diet of most ordinary people was bread, meat and beer, and for those who could not afford to buy meat very often, bread was absolutely essential. Though in these enlightened days of dieticians it is hardly a diet to be recommended, you can live for a very long time on little else but bread.

During the Middle Ages, the business of obtaining a loaf of bread was simple. The farmer threshed his corn and sent it to the miller at the windmill to be ground into flour. He then sent his sacks of flour to the nearest market and the bakers bought what they needed to make bread.

The price of a commodity always rises when it is in short supply, and in medieval times farmers were not allowed to hoard wheat in order to sell it at a high price after a bad harvest. Local justices had the power to inspect a farmer's barns and granaries and insist that he sell his stock at fair prices. There was to be no making money at the expense of hungry people. Corn sellers had to have a permit and were obliged to sell in an open market, where officials could watch and take note of the amounts of corn which were changing hands.

There were also laws against bakers who tried to sell loaves underweight. A baker who cheated was punished by being pulled around the town on a cart, with one of his underweight loaves tied around his neck, so that he looked ridiculous and all the world could laugh at him.

There was, of course, one unfortunate result of the laws against hoarding. When there was a bad harvest the country had no reserves on which to draw. This was particularly disastrous in a city like London. Before long, special granaries were built, to guard against famine in time of shortage. There was one at Leaden Hall and another at the Bridge House by London Bridge, which was placed in the care of the bridgemaster.

On one occasion, after a series of disastrous harvests, the Mayor* of London found that even the city granaries were empty, so he

* The Mayor of London was given the title of Lord Mayor during the reign of Elizabeth I.

arranged for a consignment of wheat to be sent from the Baltic port of Danzig. It arrived at the ancient port of Queenhythe, close to where the German and Flemish merchants of the Hanseatic league had been settled since about the thirteenth century, in their magnificent hall, down at the Steel Yard. Very soon, these merchants were importing regular supplies of Baltic wheat, rye and other grain, in addition to their other imports, such as cables, ropes, ships' masts, flax, hemp, linen cloth, wax and steel. They stored the corn in a big warehouse at Queenhythe and sold it to the bakers and brewers of London. But the trade was carefully watched and in time of famine they had to have a special permit to sell it.

The bakers of London seem to have settled mostly in the eastern suburb of Stratford, and carted their supplies of bread into the city each morning. Their principal markets were at Cheapside and Cornhill, and later in Bread Street, which runs off Cheapside to the south, across Watling Street to Cannon Street. In early medieval times the Stratford bakers obtained their supplies of flour from the farmers of Essex and Kent. After the fifteenth century, as London's population steadily increased, they had to go farther afield for their supplies, to Norfolk, Suffolk and Sussex. Increasing supplies of foreign corn were landed at Billingsgate and Queenhythe, though bakers seem to have preferred to buy English corn when it was in good supply.

There were various corn markets in the city but in time they were concentrated in two main areas. The first one was in Whitechapel. Essex farmers bringing their corn to London used to meet at a certain inn there. As business increased they began to leave samples of their crops with the landlord, and he took orders from the bakers and brewers who came to inspect them. The landlord would pass the orders back to the farmers and receive a commission on the sale, to pay for his time and trouble. In this way the old inn at Whitechapel became an early Corn Exchange.

Down in Thames Street, where the grain ships from the Baltic discharged their cargoes, was another inn which, in the same way, became a market for imported corn. Corn merchants who acted as brokers would buy cargoes in bulk and resell them to the bakers and brewers.

The Steel Yard merchants were expelled at the end of the sixteenth century because of complaints by the merchant adventurers that they were taking business from English traders, but foreign corn still arrived at London's quays. In 1747, a large Corn Exchange was built in Mark Lane, to house the growing businesses which the Essex farmers had begun in Whitechapel and the London merchants were transacting at Jack's coffee house. In 1827, another exchange was built next door, specializing in the sale of oats. They were separate companies with individual charters but in 1929 they amalgamated. In 1941, the exchange was destroyed by bombs but, in 1953, the present Corn Exchange, built on the old site, was opened. It is the biggest distribution point in the country for cereals and cereal products, including fertilizers and animal feeding stuffs. It is also the central market for vegetable and other horticultural seeds. British seeds are of extremely high quality. They are considered among the best in the world and are a valuable export commodity.

The Corn Exchange Company acts as a landlord, renting stands and office accommodation to dealers. It serves as a meeting place for traders in grain and all the commodities which today are associated with agriculture, as well as for shipowners and brokers, insurance-brokers who insure goods in transit, and representatives of the lightermen who transfer cargoes from the ships to the wharves, and the men who take charge of it in the riverside warehouses.

There are seven hundred firms represented on the London Exchange. Each one pays an annual subscription, in proportion to the number of members it has appointed to do business on its behalf on the Exchange. Today, there are nearly 2,000 members and the Exchange has the atmosphere of a prosperous and exclusive club, which is enhanced by the dignified beadles in their nineteenth century dark crimson uniforms.

As you pass through the comfortable members' club room, you come upon the large market hall. Here, many of the members have stands where samples of their goods are laid out on display, while others have offices in the building where they can always be found quickly for business.

There are no windows in the hall, but it is lit by a domed glass roof which gives the cold north light upon which buyers insist, in order to make a minute examination of the wares. Here in small dishes are laid out every conceivable kind of grain, feed and fertilizer, from ground oyster shells for chickens to the finest malting barley, from locust beans to guano. The salesroom is open five days a week, from ten a.m. until half-past four, but Monday mornings are usually the busiest and trading is naturally heaviest during the harvest weeks of the late summer.

Brewers and maltsters come to examine and select their requirements of barley, millers and bakers their flour and merchants their feeding stuffs and fertilizers.

Like the Baltic Exchange, the Corn Exchange is a wholesale market, but it deals in smaller quantities than those changing hands at the Baltic. Whereas at the Baltic a member might buy a whole shipload of grain, sales at the Corn Exchange can be as small as fifty tons. They are not usually more than about a thousand tons, except for the big manufacturers buying in bulk to make feeding stuffs and other products.

One of the important commodities sold on the Exchange is fertilizers. British manufacturers will buy, for example, nitrates in bulk from Chile. They use these in the manufacture of their various fertilizers, weed killers and various plant foods, which they then sell to the merchants on the Corn Exchange. Merchants come to the Exchange to buy from these manufacturers and resell to their own customers.

The old regulations controlling the tendency for a rise and fall of prices during times of scarcity and glut have emerged in a new form. Today, farming is on such a large scale that farmers could not afford to store in bulk nor would they have the space. So marketing is controlled by a body known as the Home-Grown Cereals Authority.

There are no auctions at the Exchange. All sales are by mutual agreement, known as "private treaty", and the contracts are not made by the Exchange Company at all, but by one or other of the trade associations which have offices in the buildings, or nearby, such as the London Corn Trade Association, the Cattle Food Trade Association, the Seed Trade Association and so forth.

SHIPS' CARGOES
AND GRAIN

THE BALTIC EXCHANGE

Mark Lane is one of the historic trading quarters of the City of London and was once known as Mart or Market Lane, for in ancient times an open market and a fair were held there. The Baltic Exchange in St. Mary Axe is only a short walk away. Turning right from the Corn Exchange and leaving the Tower of London and the river behind, you reach Fenchurch Street, with the imposing modern building of the Institute of Marine Engineers on the right hand corner of Mark Lane. On the left, in strange contrast, is the ancient, crumbling tower of the church of Allhallows Staining, with its graveyard turned into a gay little garden.

Turning left into Fenchurch Street, where the London headquarters of the big shipping companies are housed is Lime Street, which runs north into Leadenhall Street, and on the north side of Leadenhall Street is St. Mary Axe. It received its strange name because there was once a church to St. Mary there and also a shop, outside which hung an axe for its sign.

A few yards up the street is the Baltic Exchange, a large and dignified Edwardian building which has the same clublike atmosphere as the Corn Exchange.

The Baltic has an interesting history. By the seventeenth century, when new journeys of discovery were being made throughout the world and new markets opening, London's overseas trade in all types of commodities was increasing quickly. Much of the business connected with wholesale buying and selling took place in the city's new coffee houses.

The Virginia and Maryland coffee house in Threadneedle Street was the meeting place for merchants interested in the tobacco, sugar and cotton plantations of the American colonies, Close by, was the Baltic coffee house, where men dealing in the Russian and Baltic trade met to transact their business. By now, this trade consisted not only of grain but various other commodities. The most important of these was tallow for the candles people then used for lighting, in place of the old-fashioned rush lights. Large quantities of tallow were used, and it was a very valuable article of commerce.

In 1744, the Virginia and Maryland coffee house joined forces with the Baltic and reopened under the name of the Virginia and Baltic. By now the customers were interested not only in the cargoes, but also the ships that brought them. At the Virginia and Baltic they met the shipowners and captains and were able to keep a check on the movements of ships throughout the world and the amount of cargo space they had available at any given time. For example, a merchant wishing to send a cargo of tea and coffee to America might make arrangements with the captain of a ship sailing from the Baltic with a cargo of tallow and grain for London. After the ship had discharged its cargo in London it could be reloaded with the merchant's tea and coffee. An American merchant could have a cargo of sugar or tobacco all ready to fill the ship's hold and help pay for its return journey across the Atlantic.

This was how the "shipping" market was established and it

117

quickly became as important as any other commodity market, for it saved an enormous amount of time and money.

In 1810, the business of the Virginia and Baltic had grown too big for its old home in Threadneedle Street and it moved to the Antwerp tavern nearby, where it was renamed the Baltic. A few years later, the members formed themselves into a club, limiting their membership to three hundred. They appointed a committee to control their affairs and established a saleroom. Tallow was still the most important commodity in which they dealt, but though this was still an age of candle-light, Britain was changing very quickly. The industrial revolution had begun. By the end of the eighteenth century, the population was growing so quickly and so many people had left the land to work in the new factories, that Britain had to import increasingly large supplies of wheat from abroad.

With the outbreak of the Napoleonic Wars, these imports became extremely difficult and there was an increasing demand for home-grown wheat. The price soared. In 1793, wheat cost 50/– a quarter, and by 1812 the price had risen to 126/– a quarter.

The landowners and farmers prospered, but the wage earners on the farms and in the factories suffered terribly, as their wages did not rise with the cost of living. To prevent actual starvation, agricultural workers were given parish relief which varied with the price of bread. When a loaf cost one shilling, the workman was given three shillings a week for himself and a shilling and sixpence for each member of his family. This brought them just enough money to buy bread to keep them alive.

At the end of the war, imports of wheat were possible again, and the price of bread began to drop, as English wheat growers now had to compete with cheap wheat from Europe, America and the Empire. The Corn Laws were passed which kept the price of wheat at a fixed level. This helped the farmers, who otherwise would have faced ruin, but not the people, as the price of bread remained almost as high as ever. There was a great deal of unemployment at this time and those who had jobs received inadequate wages. Conditions did not improve for another thirty years and then, during the "hungry forties", public feeling became so strong that, in 1846, the hated Corn Laws were repealed.

Large supplies of foreign corn flowed into the country and conditions for the working people of Britain slowly improved.

It was about this time that gas-lighting was invented. The first demonstration was given in England as early as 1805 and by 1840 the Gas Light and Coke Company had been formed, prepared to carry gas wherever its pipes would reach. It meant the death of the Baltic's trade in tallow, but this was quickly replaced by the large imports of foreign wheat made possible after the repeal of the Corn Laws. Corn came from Europe and then from the rapidly developing grain-producing regions of Canada, the Argentine, the United States and Australia.

The increase in the grain trade kept pace with the increase in population. The carrying trade of the Baltic grew and this involved the organization of all the available information in regard to the movements of the world's shipping. In 1857, the Baltic moved yet again to another part of Threadneedle Street, this time to South Sea House, which had once been the headquarters of the Honourable Society of Merchant Adventurers trading to the South Seas. Sail was giving way to steam. The days of the great tea and wool clippers were numbered. In 1869, with the opening of the Suez Canal, the pattern of the old trade routes changed and the long journey to the East by way of the Cape was no longer necessary. The beautiful clippers did not disappear immediately. In fact, for another twenty years they gallantly defied the competition of the new steam boats, but by 1890 the battle was nearly over, though up till the outbreak of World War II there were a few clippers still in service and the *Pamir* made her last journey only a few years ago.

The Baltic became the world's information centre concerning the new shipping, for by now Great Britain had half the world in her hands, and was the greatest commercial and industrial power in existence. The City of London, the commercial hub of the Empire, was the heart of it all.

A similar exchange, specializing in the movements of the world's cargo steamers, had begun at the old Jerusalem coffee house on Cornhill, whose members had originally dealt in the produce of the Mediterranean and the Near East. This exchange called itself the London Shipping Exchange, and its activities overlapped with the Baltic in many ways. When both of them needed larger premises, they amalgamated. Their headquarters, known as the Baltic Exchange, were opened in St. Mary Axe in 1903.

Though today the Baltic is surrounded by a labyrinth of offices, its principal feature remains the vast floor of the exchange, on to which only members are allowed. With its marble pillars, solid mahogany doors and large central dome, it covers 20,000 square feet. The only remaining evidence of its coffee-house origins is that the attendants, in their nineteenth-century liveries, are still called "waiters", though nowadays their main function is to summon members to the telephone and deliver messages.

As at the Stock Exchange, various parts of the floor of the Baltic are informally divided into markets. In the middle is the freight market. Close by, to one side, is the air-freight market and the rest of the space is occupied by the commodity markets in grain, oil and oil seeds, including ground nuts, linseed and linseed oil, castor seeds and castor oil and soya beans.

Today, the freight market is the most important and it is concerned mainly, though not entirely, with tramp ships, as opposed to cargo liners. The owner of tramp ships leases them to trade in any part of the world where cargo needs to be carried and they are usually full of cargoes of only one commodity, such as grain, coal, iron ore or sugar. Cargo liners, on the other hand, run at regular times on regular routes, carrying whatever cargoes are available at the time they are making their journeys.

Shipping, particularly tramp shipping, is international. There are thousands of deep sea tramp ships of all nations, always ready to be chartered by any country in the world to carry cargoes; and there are merchants and shippers all over the world in need of ships to transport their goods.

The freight market of the Baltic organizes this complicated business by centralizing all the information about world shipping. Most of this comes from Lloyds, the international insurance market whose building is close by in Lime Street. News of ships and details of their arrival and departure at ports throughout the world is printed each day in Lloyd's List, which is London's oldest daily newspaper. Lloyd's Shipping Index, another daily publication, lists alphabetically some 13,000 ocean-going vessels, with their whereabouts and destinations. Each morning these details are sent to the Baltic and with this information a Baltic Exchange broker can arrange for the charter of a ship, its insurance, the insurance of the cargo, the engaging of the crew and the stevedores to load and unload it, wherever it may be. The ship may be needed to carry a consignment of fertilizers from Bremen to China or pig iron from Antwerp to Argentina and may never touch London, but the cargo will be carried and safely delivered.

Freight charges are an important item in the cost of imports and exports and this service helps to keep charges down. It means that a vessel need hardly ever travel empty, however remote its destination.

When a shipowner plans to buy a new cargo ship he has to consider not only what the cost of the ship will be but how much business it is likely to do, and this, of course, is affected by the conditions of world trade. The value of the ship depreciates from the time it is launched. Assuming it will be in service for about twenty-five years, the owner must, at the end of that time, have accumulated enough capital through freight charges to be able to replace it. His expenses in running the ship will include maintenance, fuel, wages, port dues and loading and unloading charges. From these figures minimum freight charges can be fixed. His profit comes from charges above this minimum which, as in the case of every commodity, vary with supply and demand.

At the freight market, the owner of the cargo ship negotiates with the merchant wishing to transport his goods. As the Baltic is still the largest freight market in the world, it offers the widest choice for both sides. A shipowner may agree to transport machinery from Great Britain to South America. If this journey takes place after the South

American wheat harvest, so that the ship can return with a load of wheat, instead of under ballast, his freight charges can be lower.

However, if his next chartered journey is from Cape Town to Calcutta and he can pick up a cargo in South America which is destined for Cape Town, it may be cheaper for him to refuse the wheat cargo, thus avoiding a journey to London, and go straight from South America to Cape Town. In this way he avoids a double journey across the Atlantic and also the risk that he may not be able to pick up a cargo from London for his committed journey to Cape Town.

So important are the freight charges in the export business that an exporter will sometimes study the freight market to find a ship making a journey at the most economical rate before buying a cargo for it.

Most of these transactions are made through the brokers or middlemen. The company wanting to charter a ship or shipping space will inform the chartering agent of his requirements, with the date and destination. The agent passes the word on to the chartering broker at the Baltic, who hands it on to the brokers of the shipowner's agents. The chartering agent will aim at getting the lowest rate and the shipping broker will naturally try to obtain the highest figure he can.

When a decision has been reached, it is final. Here again, as in the other City markets and exchanges, the Baltic members have a tradition of standing staunchly by their bond. A verbal agreement is as binding as one that has been put into writing.

The formal agreement is prepared and signed and a copy sent to the captain of the ship, in whatever part of the world he may happen to be, informing him what his next journey will be.

The business of freight marketing depends on the ability to see opportunities and seize them quickly. It is not quite as complicated as it might seem, for certain chartering agents are nearly always associated with specific countries and deal in their particular commodities, as for example sugar from Cuba, grain from the Argentine, Australia and North America, iron ore from Brazil, and lumber from

122

British Columbia. The agent concentrates on these areas and keeps a note of cargoes moving towards them. He is closely in touch with other agents and knows everything that is going on, including any troubles or delays which may arise.

A few firms on the Baltic arrange the sale and purchase of ships and probably half the world's business in this trade passes through the Exchange. Members of the Baltic also organize the sale of ships for scrap and will advise shipowner clients on the most advantageous time to build a ship, both from the point of view of time of delivery and the price. Brokers also give evaluations of ships, for insurance and for salvage.

The Air Freight Charter market at the Baltic is growing in importance every year. It began soon after the war in a small way, carrying perishable goods such as fruit, flowers and fish, but now it has developed for both passenger transport and relatively heavy cargoes. Today the Baltic Airbrokers' Association is becoming recognized as a world market for the charter of aircraft. The process is the same as for shipping, and is organized through brokers. The principle is that if an aircraft is required for a flight from London to, say, Karachi, it will be cheaper if the aircraft can ultimately return with a full load. This need not necessarily be from Karachi itself, but picked up on the homeward route.

Aircraft are particularly useful to shipping, and the shipping companies who helped the development of the air market use it for the quick transport of crews or the delivery of replacements of machinery which may suddenly become necessary.

Charter flights are arranged for various groups of people, delegates to overseas conferences, pilgrims to Mecca or just parties of tourists going for a summer holiday.

At a rough estimate, the world seaborne trade today is 1,550,000,000 tons, of which oil represents 55%. Excluding oil, about 100,000,000 tons is carried on the open freight markets of the world, and it is thought that the Baltic handles about 60% of this total.

Of the commodity markets at the Baltic, grain is the most vital, for despite rising home production Great Britain still has to import

8,000,000 tons of grain each year. 55% of this is wheat and the remainder coarse grains such as maize and barley.

The seven main grain importing cities are London, Liverpool, Bristol, Hull, Glasgow, Leith and Belfast. Each has a Port Corn Trade Association, affiliated with the National Federation of Corn Trade Associations.

The trade is divided into shippers and their agents, who buy grain in overseas markets and who act as agents for overseas organizations, on the one hand, and the importing merchants and manufacturers on the other. Between these two sections the brokers act as the negotiators.

The grain market at the Baltic is very different from the Corn Exchange, as the actual grain is never seen here, the Baltic being concerned with the business side of importing. Sometimes, United Kingdom traders will buy all the grain that a country has to export. The business of shipping these huge quantities as efficiently and cheaply as possible, and at the same time keeping a continuous supply of grain available for British consumption, is both complicated and skilled.

In a corner of the Exchange is what is known as the Grains Futures Ring. This is an octagonal wooden rail, rather like an outsize umbrella stand, about ten feet across and standing at waist level. At 11.30 each morning, a gong is struck and members of the Ring gather round to make bids for barley and maize. The Futures market in wheat was closed at the outbreak of the last war and has never yet reopened.

Trading is from 11.30 a.m. until 1 p.m., and again from 2.45 p.m. until 4.15 p.m. The Ring would appear to be nothing more than a convenient bar on which to lean, but in practice, by gathering around in the way they do, members have a clear view of each other's faces and expressions, which at times can be useful to a shrewd buyer.

As prices are fixed across the Ring they are recorded on a board and broadcast to the world by brokers and press agencies.

"Futures" contracts must always be made at the price which has been fixed across the Ring and the difference or margin between this price and that at which the contract for some "futures" delivery has been made must be paid up the same day.

The other important commodity markets on the Baltic are oil and oil seeds and they are marketed from every producing country in the world. Crushed oil seeds are a vital ingredient for cake and meal for feeding cattle, pigs, sheep and chickens. Members of the Baltic dealing in the import of these oil seeds are often also members of the Corn Exchange, where they sell their finished manufactures.

Of the numerous types of oil imported, linseed oil is the main ingredient in the manufacture of paint and linoleum, of which Great Britain exports considerable quantities. Groundnut oil, cotton seed oil and palm kernel oil are some of the principal ingredients of margarine and cooking fats.

Only a few doors from the Baltic stands the fascinating little church of St. Andrew Undershaft, one of the few city churches to escape destruction in the great fire of 1666. Here, until early in the sixteenth century, a long shaft or Maypole was set up every May day. The Baltic Exchange and Lloyd's, both being in the parish, have always had a close connexion with the church and contribute to its upkeep, while for many years the secretary of the Baltic Exchange has been one of the church wardens. The most interesting monument in the church is that of John Stow, the son of a tallow chandler who became one of London's most famous historians. He was born in 1525 and died in April, 1605. His monument in St. Andrew Undershaft, where he regularly worshipped, shows him seated at a desk, with an open book before him and a quill pen in his hand. Every year, about the time of his death, the Lord Mayor, amongst his many other duties, pays tribute to the memory of wise and kindly old John Stow by placing a fresh quill in his hand.

COTTON

THE LIVERPOOL COTTON EXCHANGE

Mankind has spun and woven cotton for thousands of years. China, India, Egypt and Mexico each claim to have been the first to have used it. But fragments of cotton cloth, which were at least four thousand years old, have been found in the Middle East, and pieces which were probably even older have turned up in the excavations at Ur of the Chaldees in the lower valley of the Euphrates.

There are records of a few bags of cotton being imported into England in the eleventh century, but at that time, and for many years to come, English spinners and weavers used only flax and wool. By the beginning of the seventeenth century, cotton was being imported to London in small quantities by the Levant trading company to make wicks for candles. Then, with the development of English colonies in the West Indies and America more cotton was imported, for in the West Indies the cotton plant was found growing wild. Since, at this time, there was a shortage of flax, some of the Lancashire spinners experimented with cotton.

Its popularity grew and at most of the west coast British ports, as well as London, a few bags of cotton would be landed, together with sugar, rum, tobacco and coffee, which were the main commodities of the West Indian trade.

The cotton industry grew steadily in south Lancashire, and Manchester merchants travelled with increasing frequency to London and the various west coast ports to buy cotton. They took it back to Manchester to be stored in their warehouses. They could thus distribute it to the industry as it was needed and keep the workers steadily supplied.

The damp climate of Lancashire was particularly suited for the handling of cotton and, before long, Liverpool had become the principal port for its import. In June, 1757, the first cotton auction in Liverpool was announced. "To be sold by auction, at the Merchants' Coffee House, on Thursday, the 16th inst., at one o'clock precisely. 28 bags Jamaica Cotton in four lots. Samples to be seen with R. Robinson, Broker."

Those twenty-eight bags represented 6,720 lbs. of cotton. It was the beginning of the Liverpool Cotton Market.

For many years before this, with the development of European colonies in the New World, Negro slaves had been imported from West Africa to work on the new plantations. Now Liverpool was to become involved. As the taste for cotton cloth grew and the industry around Manchester boomed, a triangular trade grew up between Liverpool, West Africa and the West Indies. These instructions issued in 1762 to the master of the *Marquess of Granby*, about to set sail for West Africa, show how the business worked.

". . . Purchase 550 slaves and lay out £400 in Ivory. Pray mind to be very choice in your slaves. Buy no distempered or old ones . . . after reaching the Leeward Islands (sell the slaves) Guadaloupe or Martinico, or any other of the Leeward Islands whichever is the best market . . . and to have the ship loaden in the following manner: Viz: about one hundred casks good Mus Sugar for the Ground Tier, the remainder with the First and Second White Sugars, in betwixt Decks with good Cotton and Coffee . . . Proceed to Jamaica . . . then have the ship loaden in the following manner: Viz: as much Broad Sound Mahogany as will serve for Dunnage, the Hold filled with the very best Mus Sugar and Ginger and Betwixt Decks with Good Cotton and Pimento and about Ten Puncheons Rum . . ."

Generally the slaves were bought from African chiefs and their dealers, who sold mostly condemned prisoners or captured enemies, at least in the early days of this grim business. They explained that as the prisoners would have otherwise been put to death, they were really doing every one a good turn by selling them. They received in exchange brightly coloured Manchester cottons, the most popular being bright blues and greens, which they used for robes and loin cloths. The British ships, laden with slaves and other West African commodities, mainly gold dust, ivory and spices, set off westward, taking the stormy "middle-passage" across the Atlantic to the West Indies. There they sold the slaves for cash, bought their supplies of cotton, sugar, coffee and rum and set sail once more for Liverpool.

The slave trade was abolished early in the nineteenth century, by which time England's industrialization was under way and the Western World was changing rapidly. Like the woollen industry of Yorkshire, the Lancashire cotton industry, based around Manchester, expanded very quickly. By now America had become the chief cotton-producing country and Liverpool was the largest raw cotton importer in the world.

The marketing of cotton was similar to that of the commodities being imported to London. Brokers bought from America and the other producing countries, including the Levant, the West Indies, Brazil and India. They stored the cotton in their warehouses and periodically sold it by auction on their own premises.

To cover the risk of loss through cotton prices dropping during the long voyage across the Atlantic, a method of forward buying began which was to develop into a "futures" market in cotton. This method of marketing developed in Liverpool and was later adopted at the Baltic and other London commodity exchanges.

Increasing varieties of cotton arrived at Liverpool and were sold by the brokers to Manchester spinners, who, in the early days, arrived by stage coach in Liverpool. They sent the cotton back to their factories by horse-drawn wagons, but the building of the Manchester Ship Canal in the 1760's eased the transport problem and reduced freight charges.

In 1770, there were only two stage coaches a week running between Liverpool and Manchester, but, by 1800, there were seventy, and the inns surrounding the stage coach terminal in Liverpool, around about Castle Street, prospered with the rapidly increasing business. At this time more than 60,000,000 lbs. of cotton were arriving each year in Liverpool, and large quantities of manufactured cloth were being carried from Manchester to Liverpool for export.

It was Mohammed Ali who, early in the nineteenth century, introduced the cultivation of cotton in the Sudan and authorized improved irrigation methods which greatly increased the yield. Cotton became an important source of wealth both to Egypt and the Sudan, and consignments of this high quality cotton were soon arriving at Liverpool.

Although the Liverpool Cotton Market was by now so important, it still had no central organization and was composed of a number of individual brokers and merchants who used to meet regularly at the top of Castle Street and transact all their business in the open air. This caused endless traffic jams amongst the carriages and carts and annoyance to the rest of the citizens of Liverpool.

In 1795, the old Liverpool Exchange was burned to the ground and when the New Exchange, later to become the Liverpool Town Hall, was built, the cotton merchants were offered accommodation there. Though they still preferred to do their business in the open air, they now moved to the open space in front of the Exchange, known as "the flags". Here the different brokers took up their stands, including the traders specializing in "futures" sales.

This was all very well when the weather was good but on wet days the cotton merchants were forced to take cover under the surrounding arcades. The "futures" prices were posted on one of the pillars as they were announced, and kept on display while the market was open for business. Traders kept a record of transactions and at the end of the day's business, when they returned to their offices close by, contracts were made out and sent to all the market firms concerned.

Trading in the open air like this was often fast, noisy and exciting and was a popular show for visitors. The merchants, well aware of the fact that they were providing good entertainment, took great pride in their appearance and became known as the best-dressed business men outside the City of London.

Even the "futures" market remained in the open air for many years, the traders forming themselves into a ring, so that they could make their bids and acceptances more clearly and easily.

The railway between Liverpool and Manchester was opened in 1830 and after that time all cotton buying was concentrated in Liverpool. By 1832, Liverpool became the biggest importing raw cotton market in the world and the members of the market began to organize themselves. The Liverpool Cotton Market was composed of the buying brokers, representing the spinners, and the selling brokers, representing the importers.

In 1841, the Liverpool Cotton Brokers Association was formed, composed of ninety firms. This was replaced in 1882 by the Liverpool Cotton Association. Yet the dealings still took place in the open air, on "the flags".

With the arrival of the telegraph and then the telephone and the general speeding up of marketing, with the rapid reporting of news and prices, this open-air marketing became impractical. In 1896, the "futures" market moved into Brown's Buildings, overlooking "the flags" and merchants concerned with the day-to-day selling of cotton moved to offices close by.

However, business in cotton increased so much that in 1903 the large and dignified Liverpool Cotton Exchange was built. The central feature of the building was the main Exchange Room with its central Cotton Ring, surrounded by four tiers of seats for the traders in the "futures" market. In the rest of the Exchange were the offices and

130

sale rooms of the member firms, where most of the business in cotton was conducted.

This was the peak of prosperity for the Lancashire cotton industry. After the First World War, the trade began to suffer from competition by the textile manufacturing countries of the East and during the Second World War conditions became desperate. Not only were cotton supplies interrupted by the Atlantic German U-boat campaign, but Liverpool itself was terribly damaged, particularly in 1941, during eight nights of intensive bombing.

Cotton supplies were so insecure that the "futures" market closed. The government took charge of the buying and distribution of cotton, and it was not until 1953 that the Liverpool Cotton Market was reopened. Though there are opportunities for "futures" dealings in American and Sudanese cotton, the "futures" market is not very active nowadays. The Association no longer owns the Cotton Exchange Building though they still have premises there. Membership of the Exchange must be by election and the payment of an annual subscription. The old floor where the "futures" trading took place has been demolished and new offices built in its place.

As British markets for Lancashire cotton have diminished, with increasing competition from other cotton-manufacturing countries— particularly since 1952—the importance of the Liverpool Cotton Exchange has declined. In 1911, five and a half million bales of cotton were imported at Liverpool, but today the figure is about one and a half million.

Like the woollen industry, the cotton industry has also suffered from the competition of man-made fibres. In 1964, the value of the exports of cotton yarn and woven cotton fabrics was £44.1 million. The principal markets were Australia, South Africa, the Irish Republic and New Zealand. But the value of exports of man-made fibre yarns and woven fabrics was £58.5 million, and the principal markets were Sweden, the Republic of South Africa, Australia, the Irish Republic and Switzerland.

Nevertheless, although the importance of the Liverpool Cotton Exchange has declined in regard to imports to the United Kingdom, certain Liverpool firms carry on a very large business in cotton which never reaches Britain. For example, a Liverpool firm may buy cotton in the United States of America and sell it to Japan, the cotton travelling directly across the Pacific. As the profit from such a transaction comes to the United Kingdom, this trading may be described as an invisible export.

A Lancashire mill lass   Photo: C.O.I.

WORLD PRODUCE

THE LONDON COMMODITY EXCHANGE

During the early part of the reign of Queen Elizabeth I, in the middle years of the sixteenth century, there lived in Lombard Street, in the City of London, Sir Thomas Gresham. He was a financier and merchant who did business with Antwerp, the Netherland city which was at the height of its wealth and power. Antwerp received each year, from London alone, woollen cloth worth over a million pounds. Into London, in exchange, came all manner of luxuries, including precious stones, cloth of gold and silver, silks and velvets, spices, drugs, sugar, cotton, tapestries and Oriental carpets, glass, metalware, arms, household furniture and rare perfumes and essences, collected in Antwerp from all over Europe and many parts of Asia.

As in Venice, there was a large exchange in Antwerp, where foreign goods could be displayed to prospective buyers; but when the Spanish armies began their conquering advance across Europe the days of Antwerp's prosperity were numbered. As Sir Thomas watched

An auction in progress in the coffee section of the Exchange   P. F. Crawshaw

her gradual eclipse, he planned to direct Antwerp's business and financial dealings to London.

London merchants displayed the goods they imported from the Continent as best they could in their own dark houses and warehouses. They were built along Thames Street and Tower Street and the little streets which ran down to them from Fenchurch Street, particularly Mincing Lane where once stood the houses of the minchins or nuns of St. Helen's, Bishopsgate, and Market or Mark Lane.

Sir Thomas Gresham planned a market which would rival Antwerp and even the old Venetian bourse. A site was cleared in the heart of the City, where Cheapside and Poultry, Threadneedle Street and Cornhill meet. The first exchange was built, which Queen Elizabeth later named the Royal Exchange. It was a large building with a double balcony, built around a courtyard surrounded by a covered walk supported by marble pillars. Here there were a hundred shops and twice a day, at noon and six o'clock in the evening, a bell was rung summoning merchants to hear the news of the day and transact business. Grocers and druggists, apothecaries and goldsmiths, booksellers and glass-sellers, milliners and haberdashers displayed their goods at the Royal Exchange. It became a fashionable meeting place and the impetus to London's overseas trade was tremendous. Stow tells us that the Exchange was "crowded with merchants, grave and sober men, walking within in pairs, or gathered in little groups. Amongst them were foreigners from Germany, France, Venice, Genoa, Antwerp and even Russia, conspicuous by their dress."

Gresham's Exchange was destroyed by the Great Fire of 1666 but it was rebuilt and open for business again by 1670. Merchants in particular trades had their own part of the floor, called "walks", where they met each other to buy and sell, by sample, the bulk of their goods being still stored in the riverside warehouses.

With the opening of the coffee houses a few years later, however, merchants gradually deserted the Royal Exchange. Very soon individual coffee houses became associated with distinctive groups of merchants dealing in particular kinds of merchandise. As well as providing food and drink and newspapers for these merchants they often had a saleroom where their commodities could be auctioned.

At Edward Lloyd's coffee house in Tower Street, the business of marine insurance developed and grew so large that Lloyd's ultimately moved back into the Royal Exchange, where they remained until 1928, when they moved to Leadenhall Street and the new building in Lime Street.

136

As more and more foreign produce arrived in London, with increasing exploration and travel and the development of overseas markets, London merchants and their brokers made connexions with all parts of the world and began to establish their own overseas agents. More warehouses were built near the river, where goods were sampled, graded and catalogued for auction. The merchants themselves also financed the building and equipment of merchant vessels, all of which had to be armed. Even when Britain was not officially at war, foreign privateers were usually on the prowl, and pirates, who worked for no one but themselves, were always a hazard.

The merchants of London sent their ships across the seven seas to seek new merchandise for sale in London. Once it arrived, they quickly found a sale for it and paid the owners. The City merchants established a tradition of prompt payment and good trading which made merchants and planters all over the world eager to send their goods to London.

The India and China trade was, for many years, in the hands of the East India Company and they stored their goods and held their sales on their own premises. All the merchandise from the West Indies, including sugar, rum and coffee, was transported in British ships to London. The merchants involved in this trade met and auctioned it in the Jerusalem coffee house and Garraway's. Both these coffee houses were burned down in 1748. It was the end of the Jerusalem, but Garraway's was rebuilt and for many years to come was famous for its auction sales of foreign produce. Then, in 1811, the London Commercial Sale Rooms were opened in Mincing Lane, and in 1863 Garraway's closed. The new Sale Rooms formed a central exchange for the marketing of produce which had not a special market of its own, such as the Wool Exchange or the Corn Exchange. West Indian sugar was its most valuable market at first, as at that time sugar was Great Britain's largest import. Sugar sales were from samples and large amounts were re-exported.

Eight million gallons of West Indian rum were imported each year, a good deal for re-export, but the large quantities of West Indian coffee which came in were mainly for home consumption.

Other commodities handled on the Exchange included tallow, wines, barks and shellacs, which are resins used in varnish. When the East India Company's monopoly was brought to an end in 1833 and the trade was free for all, the tea sales were transferred to Mincing Lane, too. The ancient spice market was also established here.

The Sale Rooms were completely destroyed during an air raid in 1941, and the members were invited to move to Plantation House close by, the home of the London Rubber Exchange. Plantation House had been opened in Mincing Lane in 1936 and in this great building the London Commercial Sale Rooms became established as the London Commodity Exchange.

Like its predecessors, the Royal Exchange and the Commercial Sale Rooms, the London Commodity Exchange is a market place where traders meet to transact their business. The heart of the establishment is the exchange room, but around and above it are literally hundreds of offices belonging to the numerous trade associations connected with the various commodities which are sold on the "floor". The Exchange is run by a board of directors helped by the "floor" committee, who manage the exchange room where the buying and selling take place. The directors have no control over the methods or conditions of trading in the various markets, however. Like other market authorities, they provide the premises and the services. These include a Reuter's ticker service, recording up-to-the-minute commodity prices in the principal world markets and the most up-to-date telephone service in the City of London, which can handle nine hundred calls in an hour.

The buyers and sellers work under the rules of their own trade associations. Tea is the only market on the Exchange which regularly sells by auction, in its salesroom on the top floor of the building.

The commodities in which merchants deal today on the Exchange include rubber, sugar, coffee, cocoa, shellac, jute, copra, gums and waxes, vegetable oils and oilseeds, essential oils and spices, and most of these are sold by private treaty.

In the tradition of the Baltic and also the Stock Exchange, each market is concentrated on a particular part of the floor of the

Exchange and here the traders gather at any time between 10 o'clock in the morning and 5 o'clock in the afternoon, from Mondays to Fridays.

The rubber market is very important. Rubber is obtained by solidifying the white liquid or "latex" which exudes from the trees and shrubs of the rubber plant family. The trees are tapped and a certain amount of the latex is exported in this liquid form. At Tilbury docks, about half a mile upstream, is a jetty with a pipe line, by means of which liquid latex can be piped ashore from the ship to storage tanks. Usually, however, latex is converted into standard sheets of rubber before it is exported.

When the consignment of rubber is ready for shipment, the plantation company informs its London agent. More than likely, the consignment has already been bought. If not, the agent will either go to his usual dealer, giving him the necessary details of the quantity of rubber, the name of the ship and the date of its arrival or, if he has no buyer in view, he will approach his broker on the Rubber Exchange and ask him for a price. This he may accept. If not, he will wait until the price, which varies with supply and demand, is more advantageous.

The broker is not allowed to buy it for himself and hold it for resale at a more propitious time. He may buy only if he has a dealer ready to take the rubber. It is not always easy for the supplies of rubber to be regulated to the rate that manufacturers are ready to buy it, and it is the dealers who buy any surplus for a later sale. When prices are rising and falling very quickly, he may stand to lose or gain, and this is why there is a "futures" market in rubber, similar to that on other commodity exchanges.

Warehouse stocks are not particularly large. However, with the co-operation of the four sections of the Rubber Trading Association, the producing companies, the importers, the brokers and the independent dealers, the supply from the plantations to the manufacturing companies keeps flowing fairly smoothly.

The London Rubber Market is not as large as before the 1939 war as markets have developed near the production areas, as at Singapore,

139

Colombo and Djakarta. There is also an increasing tendency for manufacturers to buy direct from the producers through their own buying organizations. However, London is still unchallenged as the "futures" market, and dealers from Singapore to New York will use this device of the London market to protect themselves.

Some countries do not use brokers in these market dealings. The broker came into existence in the days when travel was slow and difficult and he acted as the "man on the spot" to save both buyer and seller the time and money involved in a long journey. Today, most British traders still prefer to use brokers. They are bound to secrecy and link the buyer and seller without ever disclosing their identities. Through their trade associations, the selling broker guarantees the quality of the goods and the buying broker the payment. And if there is any default on either side, the organizations are able to make redress. So the use of a broker is as good as an insurance.

On the Commodity Exchange there are also "futures" markets in cocoa, sugar, coffee and shellac.

Cocoa is a very old market. It was first brought back to Spain by Cortez and reached England in 1656, a few years earlier than either coffee or tea. Early in the present century, the British Government introduced the plant to the Gold Coast (now Ghana) and, by 1920, the Gold Coast was exporting more than half the world's consumption. Great Britain is a large consumer of cocoa and its products. In fact the English eat more chocolate and sugar confectionery than any other people. In 1964, Britain produced 633,000 tons of chocolate and sugar confectionary and exports of cocoa preparations, including chocolate—most of which went to Canada and the United States of America—amounted to over £10,000,000.

A chocolate manufacturer will want to know several months ahead how much his cocoa and sugar supplies are going to cost him. This enables him to make plans without the risk of losing money if anything goes wrong with the crops, and prices rise with sudden shortages. He will, therefore, instruct his broker to buy ahead for him at the Commodity Exchange.

The prices in these "futures" markets are fixed amongst the dealers across the "ring" as at the Baltic Exchange, and the final figures marked on a blackboard for everyone to see.

In the spice market, where sales are by private treaty, white pepper, once known as "grains of Paradise", is perhaps the most important item. It comes from the berries of a shrub found throughout many parts of the tropics, but the bulk of the world's supply comes from the Far East. Cayenne pepper comes from the pods and seeds of capsicum plants. Cardamons, used in making curry powder, are indigenous to Malabar and Ceylon. Cassia and cinnamon, cloves and ginger, nutmegs and mace all arrive at the London docks and are stored in the warehouses there until they are needed. Then samples are taken to the brokers' sale rooms at the Exchange, inspected by buyers and bought on the spot, either for home consumption or re-export.

Spices are only one of a vast assortment of valuable commodities which are stored in the City warehouses. In 1909 the Port of London Authority took over the enormous Cutler Street warehouses, just off Houndsditch, which had been built between 1765 and 1782 for the old East India Company. They cover five acres and have a floor space of more than 600,000 square feet. A large part of the accommodation is now used for the storage of valuable Eastern carpets. There are a hundred rooms full of the loveliest and most precious carpets from India, China, Persia and Turkey, for this is the world market for Eastern carpets, many of which are bought for re-export. At times, there may be a hundred thousand carpets and rugs stored in Cutler Street, but there is ample room for buyers to inspect them, and in the surrounding streets are the offices of the London carpet merchants, most of whom are Armenians.

There is a huge basement with double-locked double doors for medicinal drugs—including opium—which are ultimately bought by the big manufacturing chemists.

Ostrich feathers, ivory and tortoiseshell are all stored in the Cutler Street warehouses and, from time to time, they are traded on the London Commodity Exchange.

On another floor, cigars from Jamaica and Havana are stored, along with other manufactured forms of tobacco. These have to be weighed and repacked for the Customs. But unmanufactured tobacco from America, South Africa, India, Greece and Turkey, as well as a variety of commodities, including sugar, coir mats, cased wines and spirits are stored at the Commercial Road warehouse close by.

Within recent years facilities have been provided at Cutler Street for the bottling and storage of nearly 1,000,000 bottles of wine until they reach maturity.

When John Masefield visited Cutler Street early in 1914 he wrote these lines to commemorate his visit:

> "You showed me nutmegs and nutmeg husks,
> Ostrich feathers and elephant tusks,
> Hundreds of tons of costly tea,
> Packed in wood by the Cingalee,
> And a myriad drugs which disagree.
> Cinnamon, myrrh, and mace you showed,
> Golden Paradise birds that glowed,
> More cigars than a man could count
> And a billion cloves in an odorous mount,
> And choice port wine from a bright glass fount.
> You showed, for a most delightful hour,
> The wealth of the world and London's power."

A half century and two world wars later there have been incalculable changes. Britain's power has declined, but her markets, with their tradition of fair trading and integrity, survive and flourish.

142

I am greatly indebted to: the Superintendents of Billingsgate and Leadenhall, Smithfield and Spitalfield markets; the Covent Garden Market Authority; the secretaries of the Baltic Exchange, the Corn Exchange, The Metal Exchange, the London Commodity Exchange, London Wool Brokers Limited, The Liverpool Cotton Association, Limited, the Fur Trade Association, the Tea Brokers' Association of London and Brooke Bond and Company Limited.

Their kindness and help during the writing of this book has been invaluable. The time they have so generously given in reading and checking the manuscript has enabled me to give as clear and accurate a picture as possible of market conditions at the present time.

I am also most grateful to them for permission to reproduce many of the photographs.

M.C.B.

*   *   *   *

Table showing comparative values of U.S., Australian and New Zealand dollars against the pound sterling.

		1d.	6d.	1s.	£1
	U.S.	2c.	12c.	24c.	$5.00
1936	New Zealand*	0.01	0.06	0.12	$2.50
	Australian*	0.01	0.06	0.12	$2.50
	U.S.	1c.	7c.	14c.	$2.80
1952	New Zealand*	0.01	0.05	0.10	$2.00
	Australian*	0.01	0.06	0.12	$2.50
	U.S.	1c.	6c.	12c.	$2.40
1968	New Zealand	0.01	0.05	0.11	$2.14
	Australian	0.01	0.05	0.11	$2.14

* The Australian and New Zealand dollars were introduced in 1966 and 1967, respectively.

143

BIBLIOGRAPHY

Britain: Official Handbook, H.M.S.O. 1966. Sir Oscar Hobson, *How The City Works*, News Chronicle, London, 1959. W. J. Passingham, *London's Markets*, Sampson Low and Company Limited, 1935. Edward Walford, *Old and New London*, Cassell and Company Limited, 1890.

Central Markets and *About Billingsgate*, both published by the Corporation of London. *Covent Garden Market*, published by the *Covent Garden Market Authority*.

Spitalfields Market and *Nature's Bounty of Fresh Fruit and Vegetables*, both published by the Corporation of London. The *Cape Sun* issue dated June, 1967.

The Legends and History of Tea, The Story of Tea—Growth and Manufacture, The Story of Tea—Packing and Distribution, The Cultivation and Manufacture of Tea in China, The Enchanted Island— Ceylon, all published by Brooke Bond and Company Limited in 1966 and 1967. *How Ceylon Tea is Grown and Marketed*, published by the Ceylon Tea Centre and *London Tea Auctions*, published by the *Tea Brokers' Association*.

Facts about Pure New Wool, published by the International Wool Secretariat; *Selling Wool on the London Market*, published by the London Wool Brokers.

Fur Trade Facts, published by the Fur Trade Information Centre.

The London Metal Exchange, published by the Economist Intelligence Unit, Limited, 1958. *The Evolution of the London Metal Exchange*, published by the London Metal Exchange, 1967.

The Baltic Exchange and *The Markets of the Baltic Exchange*, both published by the Baltic Exchange.

Liverpool Raw Cotton Annual, 1957 and 1958, Cotton and the Liverpool Market, all published by the Liverpool Cotton Association, Limited.

Port of London—Notes for Students, published by the Port of London Authority. *Notes on the London Commodity Exchange*, published by the London Commodity Exchange Company, Limited.

Printed in Great Britain by John Gardner (Printers) Ltd.
Liverpool, 20

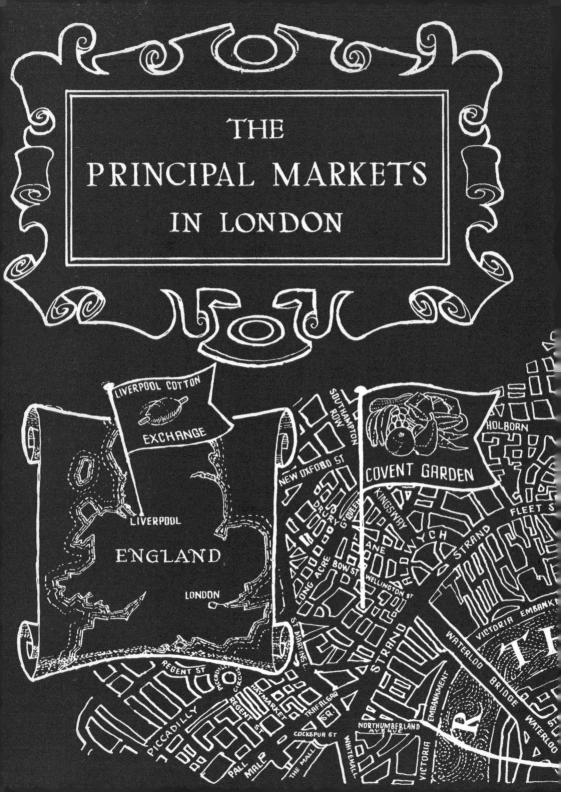